PENGUIN BOOKS

THE LAST DRAFT

Sandra Scofield is the author of seven novels, including *Beyond Deserving*, a finalist for the National Book Award, and *A Chance to See Egypt*, winner of a Best Fiction Prize from the Texas Institute of Letters. She has written a memoir, *Occasions of Sin*, and a book of essays about her family, *Mysteries of Love and Grief: Reflections on a Plainswoman's Life.* Her most recent book of fiction is *Swim: Stories of the Sixties.* She is also the author of a previous book on the craft of writing, *The Scene Book: A Primer for the Fiction Writer.* Scofield is on the faculty of the Solstice MFA Program in Creative Writing at Pine Manor College and has for many years taught at the University of Iowa Summer Writing Festival. She lives in Missoula, Montana, and Portland, Oregon.

THE
LAST DRAFT

A Novelist's Guide to Revision

SANDRA SCOFIELD

PENGUIN BOOKS

PENGUIN BOOKS

An imprint of Penguin Random House LLC
375 Hudson Street
New York, New York 10014
penguin.com

LIBRARY OF CONGRESS CATALOGING-IN-PUBLICATION DATA

Names: Scofield, Sandra Jean, 1943– author.
Title: The last draft : a novelist's guide to revision / Sandra Scofield.
Description: New York : Penguin Books, [2017]
Identifiers: LCCN 2017032030 (print) | LCCN 2017041432 (ebook) |
ISBN 9781524705084 (ebook) | ISBN 9780143131359 (softcover)
Subjects: LCSH: Fiction—Technique. | Fiction—Authorship. |
Manuscripts—Editing. | Creative writing. | BISAC: LANGUAGE
ARTS & DISCIPLINES / Composition & Creative Writing. |
REFERENCE / Writing Skills. | LANGUAGE ARTS &
DISCIPLINES / Editing & Proofreading.
Classification: LCC PN3365 (ebook) | LCC PN3365 .S38 2017 (print) |
DDC 808.3—dc23
LC record available at https://lccn.loc.gov/2017032030

Printed in the United States of America
1 3 5 7 9 10 8 6 4 2

SET IN ADOBE CASLON PRO
Designed by Katy Riegel

I love the flowers of afterthought.

—Bernard Malamud

Contents

Introduction

Why you, why me, why this book?

We're an odd lot, novelists. Obsessive. Why else does someone
launch a project that consumes so much time and holds out
such a wavering promise of reward? I wrote my first three novels in deep night—the only time I had—and I used to put
things away (in a dish bucket, set against the kitchen wall) in a
tired heave of sadness, as if I might never pick them up again,
as if my fledgling world might never be real. And of course it
never was, because that's a large part of the siren call of the
novel: Come hither and create your own world. Put what you
know and believe and want into story. Defy the randomness of
real life; make meaning. This is a long-haul project and it is so
much a part of who you are, you can't imagine not doing it, not
even if it takes years.

Maybe you, like me, write in your hidey-hole and people
who know you have no idea how much you've taken on. Maybe
you've found a workshop or a graduate program to help you in
your endeavor. Either way, you must know by now that you
have a world of figuring out to do.

Just know this: You are uniquely you, and the novel you write is one nobody else can.

I've written seven novels. That doesn't count the first one; I spent years, only to discover when it was done that I was sick of it. (I had learned a lot, though.) It doesn't count the one I lost. (I thought I stored it in the linen closet, but it wasn't there when I searched for it.) It doesn't count drafts, that's for sure. It doesn't count false starts (a box of them), or the ones I've been writing in my head for a decade while I tell myself I'm done with novels. (I have been writing other things, but this book has stirred some ideas.)

I've read shelves and shelves of novels. Hundreds of reviews. (I've written them, too.) Stacks of criticism. Biographies and memoirs of writers. But what matters to the present subject is this: I have immersed myself in the struggles of at least two hundred aspiring novelists, many in one-week workshops in summer writing festivals over twenty-plus years, and others in semester-long or year-long mentorships. I immerse myself in outlines and drafts. These writers have put themselves out there in a scary, exciting way. It has been my privilege to help them find new insights and fresh resolve. There is among aspiring writers an incredible range of interests, backgrounds, sense of story, and confidence, but there are many things they have in common. They are readers. They are intrigued by human nature. They are dogged.

Since 2005 I have been teaching in low-residency master's programs, mentoring students in workshops and online. I have been coach and cheerleader. I have tried to understand what each writer is striving for, and to help that writer reach her goal. I have constructed exercises to guide the shaping of a manuscript. The opportunity to work one-on-one has been as instructive to me as it has been to my students, and workshops have been exhilarating and enlightening.

One day it dawned on me that every summer, every semester, I have reinvented the wheel. Now, going through my teaching materials, I see that, however I may have recast notes, talks, exercises, and guidelines, there are consistent themes. I want to share what I have learned in my writing and teaching life, with special gratitude for the generosity of so many writers over so many years.

First drafts: What it takes to get it down

You can find many books to help you produce the first draft of a novel, especially if you subscribe to a popular theory of story much loved by screenwriters. Their strategy of structuring with acts, journeys, plot points, and arcs seems to be ratified by the success of many commercial movies, but is less helpful in developing deep story. If you want to review the basics of screenplay structure, you should read Syd Field, who popularized the model thirty years ago. You can also find genre-specific plot guides by writers like Orson Scott Card (fantasy), James Frey (mystery), Regina Brooks (young adult), and many others. I offer my own way of seeing a writer's work, assuming that most writers accumulate advice the way painters accumulate brushes. If you are writing a first draft, the principles and strategies discussed in this book can help you think about your story. Just don't get caught up in too much self-criticism too early on. Use my ideas as prompts, not as prescription. If you do use a plot scheme to develop a first draft, this book can help you deepen your manuscript by refining your vision and intention for the story.

My advice is short and simple.

1. You should feel driven by a story you want to tell, even if you don't know every nuance of it.
2. You must be able to live with the ambiguity of the enterprise.
3. You must have a commitment to a schedule of writing.

No one can teach you how to write a perfect first draft

If you can say, Yes, I'm up to that, and you are just beginning, you may do best by ignoring instruction, at least until your dream is on the page. Free from rules, you may discover you have something in you nobody else has thought of. What rules did Markus Zusak ignore, writing *The Book Thief*, with Death as the narrator? Or Kate Atkinson, with the dazzle of her innovative *Life After Life*, in which her characters live more than one life? Amor Towles painted thirty years of Russian history in the confines of a single setting, a hotel, in *A Gentleman in Moscow*.

However much you think you know your story, however much you love it, allow yourself the freedom of discovery. Think of yourself as solving a mystery. *What if? Why?* Be wary of judging your work too soon. Sticking with a novel means going forward, not round and round. I say that even though I myself am a slow, deliberate writer at the sentence level. I don't pour out pages; I feel as if every line tells me something about what the next line has to be. But I also don't worry over the pages I've already written until I have a substantial draft. I learned early on that I could end up trying to perfect passages that don't belong in the novel at all. Or I could lose my urgency to discover *what next*. I learned to jump ahead when I felt stymied. I started two of my novels in the middle.

Keep in mind that a first draft may be a kind of fishing expedition, a mess of a manuscript. You may not be ready to leap to revising. "First draft" should be thought of as a canopy of writing, holding however many drafts it takes to get you to the place where you feel you have grasped the story and put it on the page. You have to know how it ends. You have to know what it means.

The "first draft" of my first published novel was 1,084 pages long. It took about fourteen months to write. (Remember, those were typewriter days.) I wrote ferociously and joyously. Then I had to figure out how to define reasonable parameters for the novel, and when I cut it, I discovered a huge imbalance between what I had said the most about and what I'd skimmed over. I made a painstaking outline by hand, on lined paper. There were no word processors. I had to start over with fresh paper in a typewriter. That was what it meant to revise. (I kept the boxes that held that draft in the disused cabinets over the refrigerator for many years, until they were archived. And I looked at them from time to time, a reminder of what I did, what I can do.)

When I wrote what I thought was the finished manuscript of *More Than Allies*, my perspicacious agent told me she liked a minor character in the story the best of all—and that character became one of the two main characters in a total rewrite. I learned to stay fluid, patient, open, and determined. Every stage has its hurdles—and its rewards.

Have fun finding your way

You might want to toss a chapter and start over. Fine. You might want to try out a different point of view. You could discover your heavy drama is a comedy after all. You might realize you need a lot more background (setting, history) built into the story (a common concern); or you might realize that your research is clogging the manuscript's arteries. Insight comes when you are immersed in the story, and you then have to decide whether to go back or keep going. I'm inclined to say keep going but make lots of notes about your prospective changes. You have to tell yourself that the most important thing is to get enough story down that you have something to work with; you will know more with every page you write; you can change things in the next draft.

Once you have that first full draft, you are on a different plane of writing. You've done a lot of stumbling and fretting, but you've figured out a story and you have this product, written out from beginning to end. Congratulations. Now you are ready for the next step. Unless you can do it in one go. There are writers who don't revise full drafts, but I think that for them revising is a stream of higher consciousness.

It is instructive and fascinating to read about Gustave Flaubert's writing; he was a man in agony, start to finish. He wrote letters to his friends saying that he hated what he was writing, that he had spent days on a paragraph, and so on. It seems clear to me that he had a very strong sense of his story from the beginning (I'm thinking of *Madame Bovary*), but achieving what he had in mind was incredibly demanding because his standards were so high. He spent five years writing the novel, his first. He wrote expansively, then cut, as he progressed.

When he got to the end of his "first draft," which was the complete novel, he had performed surgery, acrobatics, diplomacy, psychology, and artistry on every page. And he had written the first modern novel.

John Steinbeck wrote a journal about how he wrote *The Grapes of Wrath*. It's called *Working Days* and you can see why: He wrote five days a week, all day, from June to October 1938, about two thousand words a day. He griped and grumbled, full of self-doubt and self-pity, but he had his head down and his pencil on the paper (his wife was his typist). I think he, like Flaubert, could do a one-draft wonder because every sentence was produced from deep thought. He was driven by an urgency about his subject, and he had done a lot of research. He didn't start writing from scratch by any means.

Bernard Malamud, on the other hand, said when asked how many drafts he typically wrote, "Many more than I call three."

Fast is fast, but is it good?

So many will say, Just get it down—work intuitively and quickly. I can't write fast, so I can't evaluate this approach. Anne Lamott (*Bird by Bird: Some Instructions on Writing and Life*), famous for encouraging unself-conscious, uncritical first drafts, has made it clear that she also does a lot of restructuring and revising later on. You have to find your own way. If you have had the story in your mind for a long time, your first draft might feel like you are pouring it onto the page. If the story feels like a mystery you want to solve, it will probably go more slowly. The writer Ann Patchett (*Bel Canto*), whose novels are marvelously varied, has said that she likes to think things through pretty thoroughly before she starts writing, whereas her friend, the novelist Elizabeth McCracken (*The Giant's House: A Romance*), doesn't think a thing of changing names, histories, and plotlines as she writes. Think of the first draft as close to the chest: It's yours alone.

What I do know is that, whether you crawl through your draft or you write it out as fast as you can type, you have to have the story on the page, start to finish, before you can evaluate it. It's important to stay open to surprises and unbothered by dead ends. This isn't the time to make contracts with yourself, like so many pages a day or the first draft by Christmas. Dedicated time is the one thing you do have to promise yourself. A lot will change in the writing. Later, you will come back to the same questions, the same advice, the same exercises, and find you have gone somewhere altogether different from where you were headed. That's just fine. That's writing. The real book might appear in the margins of your draft. *You can't revise what you haven't written down.*

Rewriting

If your first draft feels clumsy or underdeveloped to you, you may just need to write another one, telling the story more fully, or telling it another way. At least now you have a story. (But before you embark on another two or three hundred pages, I urge you to try a different strategy for telling the story, and that is to develop *scenarios*, a strategy I discuss later on.)

I think of *rewriting* as something you do in an early stage of your writing project, when you find yourself giving up on the direction you've taken a scene, so you delete it and start over. You hate a paragraph. You change a character's name. You describe a setting and then decide to move the action. You're figuring it out for the first time. Most rewriting in a first draft is still intuitive, even fumbling. Computers have robbed us of a great pleasure: crumpling a page and throwing it across the room.

If you write a draft, or much of it, and realize that this is absolutely not the story you had in mind, don't try to salvage anything except the thinking you did. Don't save that perfect paragraph. Start over. Write a new first draft. Whatever shows up again should do so because it is right at the moment that calls for it, not because you didn't want to waste it. Also, if you initially have in mind that there will be a second draft, you feel freer to move along, to follow your intuition in breaking the story ground.

Are you ready to revise?

I'm supposing that readers picked up this book because of the title. You have written a draft, or most of one. You know you have work to do. I hope you already know that you don't want to jump right to fix-it mode, in which you labor over words and sentences, fix scenes, check your spelling. There's other work to be done first. You want your story to be tighter and yet more generous. You want your characters to be memorable. You want the form to fit the story like the setting for a gem. Do I dare suggest, you want your novel to say something fresh about the world? To be special?

Revision is a significantly different process because you work from a complete manuscript rather than a moving platform. Also, there is more analytical work in revision, more deliberate application of craft. I suggest you follow a process in which a period of analysis and condensed writing gives you a stronger story that moves you closer to the final version, without multiple full-length exploratory drafts. You can go back and forth between thinking about the story (re-seeing) and writing the story. It just seems too inefficient and painful to write a draft, read it and weep, and then set in writing another one, hoping it will be better. I think that's why so many novels don't get finished. The writer wears out or loses enthusiasm. Mind you, if you do have the heart for it—rewriting start to finish—it's probably the right thing for you to do. Rewriting is a more organic process than revision. Total immersion will take you back into the mine.

A caveat, from my personal experience: Using cut-and-paste on the computer as a revision strategy is a lazy and dangerous method. It means that you don't really process the text; the manuscript loses its organic integrity. Making the words go through your brain and fingers again coheres the manuscript, even if all you are doing is copying from a printed-out page. Buy ink and reams of paper, and watch your story go through its stages physically.

How to use the book

So now you are thinking: I need to revise my book. What does that mean? How do I get started?

A writer in one of my workshops recently wrote me to say:

> I realize that before the workshop I thought I would learn a few things that would show me how to magically rewrite my manuscript. Instead I learned that it isn't magic and it isn't all intuitive, either.
>
> It's a new combination of thinking about and thinking up my story.

Be sure revision is what you want to do now. Sometimes you need to put a manuscript away and do something entirely different, something physical, perhaps. Something that engages a different part of your psyche. I work with a novelist who is also a competitive swimmer; he feels his training regimen keeps him alert for his writing as much as for his swimming.

Write down why you want to revise. Is there a mystery you haven't quite solved about the protagonist? (This can be a good sign! You don't want paper dolls, flat in front with no other dimensions. Seize the challenge of your character's mystery.) Are there places that drag? Or does it go too fast?

You don't have to know what's wrong now; that's why you are going to analyze your manuscript.

STAY WITH ME as I make my first recommendation. Get away from the computer. Print out your manuscript, and as you write new material for revision, print it, too. Handle your manuscript as a real object with weight and a smell, a size, and a color. You might want to reformat the text—set line spacing to 1.5 lines, just so you don't have so many pages to handle. (But don't go overboard: Single spacing is too hard to work with.) The first thing to do is to print out a copy and bind it with coils or rings so that you can turn pages and lay them flat. That is your mother copy, to which you will often refer. Use one side only, so that you can make notes on the blank opposite page. Make a second copy and keep the pages loose, because you will be using part of it at a time, perhaps sorting it in separate sections. (I use big clips to organize chapters; it's easier to flip through thirty sets than a couple hundred single pages.) Use cheap recycled paper. I like to use a color and to have a ream of a second color on hand for new writing as I work through the draft. (You can staple old and new together as you progress, to eliminate a lot of shuffling.) You will need pens and index cards in a few colors. You might want a bulletin board and tacks, or a whiteboard and pens. I used to roll out butcher paper and tape it to the wall and write on it or tape up index cards. The point is, it helps, down the line, to have a way to create maps or charts or lists that are right in front of you. It helps to introduce physicality to the process—the opportunity to get out of the chair, to step back and see a representation of the story on the wall, to sort a stack of cards.

I've worked with writers who use Microsoft Excel or another software program to create a visual of their plot and character relationships, and they swear by it, so if you are handier than I am with the computer, you may already be onto this strategy. You can print out a spreadsheet and post it somewhere. But you still need to print out pages.

You are going to be making piles, so think about how you will manage them. If you are lucky enough to have designated space and a nice big table, piles will do fine. I have almost always worked in my kitchen, so I have several plastic dish buckets, like you get at Target or Ace Hardware. As I get going, I label them ("Draft 2," "Notes," etc.). It's easy to sort my work, to stack it neatly, bucket in bucket, and then to take it all out again the next day. And hey, there's always a little frisson of excitement, looking at all those pages.

I suggest that you keep a revision journal. Take a little time at the end of a session to write down your feelings about the day's work. List questions you don't want to forget. Summarize what you accomplished that day. Use the journal in any way that helps you remember and reflect. The act of reflecting—in writing—is an invaluable tool in revision. You are, after all, holding an awful lot in your head.

A journal helps you clarify your thinking. It is a record of your journey as a novelist: a diary, a map, an examination of conscience, a place to whine and cheer and ask questions you might answer years from now. And when you look at it a year from now—a week from now, for that matter—you'll be surprised to see what you thought, and realize that you had already forgotten it.

WORK STYLES ARE idiosyncratic, of course; take my suggestions as a model and work out your own system. But think like an architect, a carpenter, a designer, all of whom impossibly manage to do two things at the same time—grasp the whole and see the parts. Give your ideas space and someplace to land.

And one more thought: In the digital age, a lot of manuscripts become mysteries that give up their final versions but eliminate or obscure the journey of the writing. You are a serious writer; value your work and save it. On paper. The notes, the cards, the outlines. When you're done it will probably all fit in a nice manuscript box or two. (There's that cupboard space above the refrigerator!) You might want to look at it again someday. And maybe someone else will want to see it, too. That's why we have archives, so start your own.

TO REVISE A manuscript, you have to see the story in a new way. You could read it over and over until your eyes are wobbly and it would seem to be the only way you can imagine it. But if you look at it from *back there*, like a photographer with a long lens, you'll see the shape of it—the composition—and the effect. If you look at it askance, you'll notice things that seem to be there by accident, or are missing. If you take it apart you start to understand that the novel is indeed a constructed object and that you can reimagine how it is put together. What I'm doing here is giving you dozens of ways to see the novel anew. As a mature writer, you need to know how to talk to yourself about your work; if you have an editor's feedback to consider, you have to hold it against what you meant to do and what you actually accomplished. You are the expert here. Every widget is your widget.

The process of describing and analyzing a manuscript moves it away from your initial impulses so that you can decide what you like and what you don't. It raises a valuable question: *What if?* (I killed Arthur. There was a tornado. I changed the tense, point of view, or setting. I let the problem be solved earlier. I made it all happen on one day.)

Begin with description. It's a way of taking pictures of what you've built. New ideas will pop up. After that, you will find that some of my questions and exercises mean more to you than others. You'll work your way along and choose what you want to concentrate on. Your specific vision trumps my generic one: I'm talking about any novel; you are thinking about *this* novel. You'll soon recognize where you need to put your attention. The first part of the revision process, "A Close Look," is devoted to helping you describe your novel. Start with that. Don't try to fix everything in the beginning; just make notes. You are, in effect, compiling a study of your manuscript.

I suggest you read through all the sections of this book consecutively, even if you don't want to do the exercises right away. You will probably want to read some of the discussions of model novels in the Resources sections early on; choose what appeals to you. You may want to take the time to storyboard a book, a process that can be immensely valuable, especially if this is your first novel. (See Resources.)

Be patient and methodical, like a seamstress or a boat builder. You are over the hurdle of wondering if you have a story at all. You have pages you can handle. Revision has always been what I loved best in writing a novel. I hope you will, too.

Looking for help

Should you hire an editor? My response: Not yet. A first draft almost by definition is a mess of false turns and underdeveloped story. It is riddled with glitches and blank spaces. But it goes from beginning to end. It has a shape, however rough. You have the feel of the story now; you have something to work with. Begin the second draft! Clear out the weediness of your first effort, and deepen the story. You may want to do a second draft before you launch a full-scale revision. If you feel truly lost, look for a coach who can give you support step by step. Take a workshop. Join a group. Summer programs are motivating and convivial. In the graduate program where I teach, our writers stay in touch and act as readers for each other. If you can find someone like that, it can help a lot. But be wary of asking for feedback from friends who aren't writers, and of significant others. It's asking too much of them: Tell me what you think! Tell me it's good! Tell me how to fix it! I can say from experience that when a friend says the wrong thing (you don't agree; it hurts your feelings; you think she was a careless reader; what was she thinking?), it is hard to stave off resentment. It's even worse with spouses.

If you want to work with an editor, wait until you have done all you can to make the manuscript viable; the more you have accomplished on your own, the more you can get from a professional evaluation (which isn't cheap), and the less likely you are to lose your original vision. You can analyze your manuscript's strengths and weaknesses for yourself. You can take it to the next level. After you have pushed yourself as far as you can, look for professional feedback, if you are inclined. Many first-time novelists do, and so do many experienced ones. You have to be tough-skinned and open-minded; it does you little good to ask for an evaluation if you can't stand criticism, or if you aren't prepared to tackle your manuscript again.

Finding an editor isn't difficult, but you want to do all you can to find one who suits your needs and temperament. Start by defining what you want: A critique and suggestions for revision? Hand-holding as you make your way through chapters? You want an editor to spell out precisely what you can expect to receive. Editors advertise in writers' magazines and online. Jane Friedman (https://janefriedman.com) offers good advice about asking questions and talking to other clients of editors. The Editorial Freelancers Association also has useful information on its website. Always begin with a trial review—ask for a response to a scene or chapter before making a commitment to a novel. Ask for references to prior clients. And if the expense is an obstacle, consider asking for an editor's review of a portion of your manuscript—perhaps fifty pages. You should be able to learn from that what kinds of problems you are having with story and technique.

Here's the thing: If you have a story and you love writing, you can learn all the rest. You can hire a copy editor to take care of your homonym errors, your subject-predicate disagreements. But only you can think of what has to happen in your story, and only you can write it. Don't look for feedback too early, when you are vulnerable to doubt. Don't want to waste time making mistakes and hitting dead ends? Bake or garden instead.

Writing a novel is laborious. You have to have tremendous patience and commitment. I think that the reward is great. You grow as a person when you write a novel. You learn something you could discover no other way. You fulfill an inner yearning that can't be explained to anyone who hasn't had it. A dear friend of mine has written two novels, with no effort to publish either one, even though the manuscripts are good. For her, the writing was the reward, and she was happy to share it with her family and friends. I see it as an admirable demonstration of intellectual and emotional self-nourishment, as well as an avoidance of disappointment she didn't need or want to face. And I mention it as a way of saying that you can't know whether you will be published or, if you are, whether your book will sell. You can want those things to happen—so keep the reader in mind—but what will keep you going is affection for the process and your crazy mad love affair with a story.

I'm this way about painting. I do what I want because I have a vision of what I might eventually achieve and I love everything about the process. I don't ask anyone's permission or praise. I feel as if this pursuit, taken up late in my life, is unfolding and I am merely following it where it goes.

What's on offer

There is no one way to revise, no set sequence for the process. Even the same writer will find the process changes, depending on the story. There are fundamental questions, however, and there are recurring issues. My priorities in writing or evaluating a novel are: (1) clarify and deepen the vision and (2) test and strengthen the structure. In other words, the novel must have a strong, well-organized story.

In the pages that follow, I'll present vocabulary for talking about a novel. I'll talk about the process of moving from first draft to revision.

Read the sections, compile notes, write new passages, choose questions to answer and exercises to complete. I've illustrated issues with references to readily available novels that are useful models. I've chosen these books for quality and for inspiration, for staying power, for variety, and for my own feeling that what they demonstrate will help you. Though we don't know how a particular writer does what he does, we can learn a lot with close reading: What is the effect achieved? What is the demonstrated craft? *You should choose other novels to study, too*, ones that you especially admire for qualities you want to emulate, because you'll know how to read them in ways that will instruct you in your own writing. (I have used passages from my own novels, too, to illustrate points. One, because I can. Two, because I had the experience of writing them, whereas I can only guess what other writers thought when they wrote their novels. I do, however, look at novels and talk about apparent strategies, without presuming to second-guess the writers' processes.) I refer to F. Scott Fitzgerald's *The Great Gatsby* and I urge you to read or reread it. You probably read it in high school or college;

I promise you that reading it now, as a writer and a mature reader, is a whole new experience. And you should be aware that the book changed a lot in revision; indeed, Fitzgerald made changes when the novel was in proofs. The protagonist changed; the structure changed; a truer vision emerged. Any good contemporary edition of the novel should have an introduction that discusses Fitzgerald's process.

I recommend to my students that they start out by studying a good novel written for young readers, because it will teach them a lot about structure and theme. (I discuss Lois Lowry's *Number the Stars* in the Resources section.) Check awards lists, or ask a children's librarian for suggestions if you have a particular theme or age level in mind.

Read a book and then give yourself two to three hours to look at its structure: the order of events in the plot; the organization of chapters, the balance of show and tell, the openings of chapters, and the transitions. It's a low-cost self-help course that will pay off.

If you find this exercise helpful, consider doing it twice. Amass. Analyze. Learn to see the shapes of novels.

Wherever you are with your novel, if you want to assess its qualities and consider next steps, you are ready to revise.

How is this book unique?

1. It is grounded in ideas about story that allow for ambiguity and complexity, the meat of novels.
2. It isn't prescriptive, which is to say I won't make you feel you have to follow a regimen. You will find a lot of questions and ideas to make you consider what you are writing, but you will decide which issues matter most to you. You can come back to sections more than once.
3. It doesn't view revision as cutting-and-pasting and fixing, but as phases of contemplation and analysis: preparation for a new telling.

4. It assumes that you are patient and fervent, not frenzied. It assumes that you want to finish a novel and win readers, but you aren't fixated on writing a best seller that will be made into a movie. You want to find your way to tell your kind of story in the best possible way.
5. It can guide you through more than one novel—and you can adapt your process.

And maybe this is the point where I say something about myself, as in: Who are you to tell me how to write a novel? I have devoted a big chunk of my life not just to writing novels, but to studying them. As for teaching, I am by nature analytical, and I am trained in curriculum and instruction. I love teaching and my reputation is that I am practical, generous, tough, and encouraging.

I've never had a book with large sales. All my books, however, received warm critical praise, including a nomination for the National Book Award and state prizes. Believe me, I have wasted hours wondering why I didn't get a wider audience. This was before social media platforms, remember. Publishers did things to promote the books, but I remember a powerful publisher-editor blithely saying to me, "You just have to get your mojo going. Nobody knows how it happens." And I remember being *very* annoyed. Money was spent on tours, but there were never any ads, and I wished they would do more. Now I don't think that. I believe the editor was right: *The book has to get mojo and nobody knows how that happens.* I think of it like this: In every season there is a book about something nobody thought of before, or there's a star that shines on someone who didn't expect it. One writer gets a million dollars and sells poorly; another one gets a so-so contract and Oprah anoints her. The only thing we know for sure is the magic star doesn't shine on people who were *thinking* about writing a book.

What I think now is that for a book to break out it has to say something fresh. Not necessarily shocking, though it can be.

But new. All the rest of it has to be there, of course; it has to be well written. It didn't used to be like that. Lots of "old" novels were really good—but hot, innovative? I don't think that was what readers used to expect. I formed a lot of my sensibility growing up on "quiet" novels—books about relationships, about character, in a context of life much more ordinary than today's thrillers, or at least conveyed with less hysteria. Think of *Marjorie Morningstar* (Wouk), *A Tree Grows in Brooklyn* (Smith), *The Death of the Heart* (Bowen), *The Summer Book* (Jansson), *Little Women* (Alcott), *The Optimist's Daughter* (Welty). Now, though, the concept of the book—the premise—has to be one with resonance that can be talked about in sound bites. The title has to jolt you. (Read blurbs in *Oprah, Vogue, Vanity Fair, USA Today*, etc.) And it has to have something that goes right to the heart, or the gut, so that a reader just *has* to tell her friends: *Read this.* It doesn't hurt to win a Pulitzer, but in the end, there's something truly special in a book that gets passed hand to hand. That, and luck, make mojo.

Can you plan this? Well, I'm trying my best here to point out elements that matter, such as vision (your view of the world as it is or as it should be; your concept of fate). I'm pushing the idea that your story has to matter a lot to *you*. (Flaubert is the übermodel of that.) Beyond that: Read, read, read. Write the best prose you can. Be patient and work hard. *Love the process of writing and what you learn.* Make it better. When you finish one novel, begin another.

It's a different world from when I started writing novels. Writers have a lot of responsibility for their own media attention, and I'm still way behind, using only e-mail and Word. But just for the record, I feel I've had a great career. I did what I wanted to do most for a solid fifteen years; I had a splendid agent, good contracts, and a sense of accomplishment. I made a living. I didn't get famous, but I feel respected. I'm proud of my books. I've known writers who, to me, *are* famous, but who feel they didn't get the acclaim they deserved. Some died still lamenting their careers. I can only say: Get over it. Write what you love; love writing it; hope for a readership; appreciate every reader. So a million people don't buy your book? Would it be such a terrible thing to say that *only* ten thousand, or four thousand, or, hell, four hundred people read your book? Think about that. Every reader's time is precious. I love all of my readers. I thank them for what *they* gave to *me*.

And now what I love is passing on what I've learned and crossing my fingers for you.

I

The Novel: An Overview

The Novel Continuum

My students and workshop participants often refer to novels in a binary way. They think of novels as being either popular (commercial) or literary (artful). It's a false comparison that sets you up to feel defensive. And it underestimates readers.

"I want to write a book that people read!" I hear.

"I'm not going to sell out quality!" says someone else.

"I like my genre," I hear from students, as if I'm going to say there's something wrong with fantasy, crime, or romance. (In our MFA program, we have a preponderance of fantasy and crime novelists!)

But no one says, "I'm going to write schlock." No one says, "I'm writing for forty readers."

Because what we all want is to write with intelligence, imagination, and compassion. We want to be read and we want to be good. We don't expect to be read by everyone, but we have a sense of the readership we would like to have.

Back in the dark ages when I was in high school, lots of teachers graded on something called the "curve." The idea was that at one end of an imaginary line were the idiots who didn't study and who deserved F's. At the other end were the prissy nerds and natural geniuses who of course got A's. Everyone else was somewhere on the continuum between those ends, and the most common grade was right in the middle, the C. I think that approach has fallen off—I hope so—but it suggests something useful for our purposes, this idea of a continuum.

Let's forget A and F, because on our continuum we aren't making harsh judgments; we aren't going from bad to good. We're just saying that there are fewer books at each end of the line, and more as we move to the middle, which I think of as mainstream. Where most of us want to be is in the middle of this bell curve, where more books are sold. In that hump are books that have qualities from both ends—from the likely-to-be-read and the likely-to-be-respected categories. The agent Donald Maass talks about the "breakout novel" as the one that has such a powerful story that it appeals to a mass readership, while it also is written so well that it is admired for its artistry. This may mean a genre writer with a good audience writes something that a broader audience appreciates. It might mean that a literary writer with a small admiring audience writes something that appeals to many more readers. Every season, there is almost always a writer with a backlist of good books who, for whatever reason, suddenly hits the sweet spot and earns a large audience. Hilary Mantel has been turning out terrific novels for decades, but it's Thomas Cromwell who brought her fame. And of course there are writers with large audiences of readers who don't care about the issues I'm raising—they just want a good story, and they don't care that the same writers get critical attention. Anne Tyler is a prime example, with consistent best sellers *and* lots of graduate papers about her writing. Consider Jane Smiley (*A Thousand Acres*), Cormac McCarthy (*All the Pretty Horses*), and Ian McEwan (*Atonement*).

That said, not everyone wants to be in the middle. Some

writers have a very nice niche, where they write book after book for readers who seem to be lined up waiting. If that niche has a lot of book buyers, we call the book popular. If that niche garners awards and warm critical reviews, we call it literary. I think there's no reason at all to worry about where you are on this continuum, except to know what you do best, and do it. At the same time, I think that many fine literary writers want very much to enlarge their audience, and that it's a big day when they do. Think of the British writer Kate Atkinson melding mainstream sales and widespread critical praise with her novels *Life After Life* and *A God in Ruins*. She was already well-known and respected. Her most popular books were mysteries. Then she wrote two novels in which the whole idea of one person living one life was tossed out the window in favor of diced chronology and impossible history and a whole new way of conceiving of a person's time and fate, and suddenly she's both a literary star and a best seller on multiple continents. She came up with something new, and she wrote it with great craftsmanship. Justin Cronin came out of the gate with solid literary novels—and then he wrote a spectacularly successful vampire trilogy.

Or consider Stephen King, as well-known as any writer in the world, writing horror and suspense, year after year; and suddenly I'm reading reviews about how innovative he is, how he's more than a genre writer. (I think he would say he's fine with being a genre writer. Who has had a better career?)

So I'm going to chance a description of two sorts of novels, reminding you with full throat that either one is good if it's a good story, well written. And I say again that what you want is to be as good as you can be at what you do—which almost surely means drawing on both ends of the continuum. (I'll go out on a limb: I think writers of literary fiction have the most to learn from the middle, and the most to gain, but any novel is enhanced by having a resonant theme and a complex protagonist.)

Think about the novels you love; I'll bet you they can be described with phrases from both categories. Which is why this common dichotomy is ultimately a false one.

"POPULAR" NOVELS ARE usually written with a comfortable, unobtrusive voice. They are well plotted and present a question that begs to be answered. The settings can be familiar, cozy, domestic (like much women's fiction), or quite exotic. The reader easily identifies with the main character. There is clear conflict and rising action. There are surprises, but there is also a sense of inexorability. The reader is engaged, maybe reading fast, but never confused. If there is mystery, it is because it *is* a mystery. The resolution is satisfying—it has some surprise in it, but at the same time, it's just what ought to happen. There are external forces at work, often including a powerful villain, but the most interesting complications arise because of the protagonist's choices—usually in response to heightened danger or failure—which push the plot along. Memory and psychology often explain or drive character problems, sometimes simplistically (the woman abused as a child despises men; the impoverished child grows up to be CEO of a multinational corporation), and there is usually a big scene of revelation. Structure is clear, often schematic, so that the reader can follow story complications. There is always a sympathetic protagonist, but there are often alternating or multiple points of view. Some novels have almost no interiority (think of Elmore Leonard, with his rapid-fire dialogue); others are drenched in it (Jodi Picoult), appealing to different tastes in the readership. The voice of the novel may be dispassionate, focused on the action; or the voice may be highly individual, reflecting the protagonist (especially if in first person), or reflecting the diction of the writer. Scenes take up most of the real estate of the book. Read several books by a popular author and you can probably write a blueprint for writing such a novel. (Though that doesn't mean you will necessarily have the right ideas! It takes talent to write a book that has mass appeal.)

When does this kind of writing "go too far," in my estimation? When the characters are flat; they might have been lifted from somebody else's story, or from an earlier book by the same author. When the explanations for character behavior are obvious or corny or not there at all. When it's all excitement and gore, sex and burning swords, and I'm not made to care about anybody. When pop psychology is milked for explanation. When I've seen it all before. When the language is trite, dull, or, worst of all, full of errors in diction and syntax.

To be fair, though, I see two exceptions to my reservations about popular writing. One is that even though genres have apparent rules, those rules can be broken. This is much more true now than it used to be, when bodice rippers had shirtless Italian male models on the cover. When someone talented and ambitious cracks the genre with a fresh interpretation and a great voice—I'm thinking of Jennifer Weiner here—it not only means success for that writer, it means a whole new genre spreads like wildfire. Likewise, when a writer writes an entertaining novel that is totally out of his expected "territory," it is fodder for publicity: *Rich and Pretty* is an entertaining story (a "beach read") about childhood female best friends all grown up in New York City—written by Rumaan Alam, a first-generation American son of South Asian parents.

The other exception to my basic description of popular fiction is self-published books that may be riddled with glaring problems, but drenched with the kind of story there is an audience for, especially science fiction, fantasy, and romance. Hundreds of thousands of readers don't give diddly whether participles dangle or dialogue apes bad movies. They love the stories. Writers of such books seem to write spontaneously, magically, but I bet even they would be surprised at what they could do with a little more craft and reflection. Alas, they may not have time for it, or think the time worth investing.

———

"LITERARY" NOVELS SPRING from an artistic impulse. Story is usually driven more by character than by plot. There is a heightened attention to language, and often an innovative structure. There is a powerful theme, sometimes disturbing, about things that matter to the culture as well as the individual. There is a sense of largeness; the story connects with the "gift of second meaning," by which I mean that you find yourself rereading passages because you know there is something more there for you to understand. You are willing to read the book again so you can think about it more. You read a page several times because it's just so darned beautiful. You lend it to a friend, but you want it back.

Think layers. The characters are complex. The voice is unique. Memory and psychology may provide templates or motifs, but they are used with subtlety. There is a powerful premise; the story says something about the world as it is, as it could be, as it will never be. There is a strong sense of the "created world of story"; not that it isn't plausible, but somehow it's more elegant than real life. It manages, all at once, to seem both compressed and capacious. There may be a kind of authorial presence, casting philosophical light on the story and on life in general. Vocabulary is elevated. Sentence structure is varied, playful, sophisticated, or maybe crisp and clear and spare. There's more contemplation, more musing, than in a mainstream novel. Less snap.

When does this kind of novel "go too far"? When the play with language gets in the way of following a story. When the construct is too precious by far. When I get the feeling the writer didn't really care whether I could follow his thought or not. When there's so much narrator talk that I lose interest in the story, if I can find it. When it seems to be merely emulating another writer. When it's just not to my taste. Yet I could name writers who made great careers with books I found impossibly dull and arch and contrived. I have to believe that they knew what they were doing and decided early on to take what they could get, following their talents. Sure enough, they found their audience. There are so many readers, so many tastes. So many possibilities.

THINK ABOUT WHAT kind of book you want to write. Set your bar high. Draw from these descriptions the characteristics you will strive for. Really, I mean it: Make a list. Don't expect to get everything right on the first pass. You can learn to write better. I suggest as a starter list: clear, fluent, modestly adorned diction—error free, without being a smarty-pants; an idea that feels new and excites you; a well-constructed story line that comes together satisfactorily but not too early and not with tricks; someone to love; something to be afraid of; something to learn; the warmth of a storyteller's voice. Build on your strengths. If one of them isn't language, then learn to be correct. That will suffice. Make time to practice sentence craft; there are many books to help you. Find models, and practice writing passages like them. Write with restraint. Stay out of your own way.

And try this: Pick a novel you admire a lot and describe what you like. Is it reasonable to think you could write a book that had similar qualities? Or is it more likely that your eclectic taste includes books you would never write? If the second thing is true, question your assumption. Dig deeper into your own response. Maybe you are awed by the author's language and wit, but what really reaches you is a quality of the story that you could indeed aim for in your own writing. So you aren't Flaubert. That doesn't mean that you can't tell a story about a sad, foolish, passionate, deluded woman who somehow touches all of us who have impossible dreams, if that's the story you have in you. You aren't Cormac McCarthy. But maybe you believe that boys become men when they survive harsh adventure, and you know an adventure that would make a heck of a story. Maybe you are in love with the quotidian—you think everyday life is full of muted drama and that's what captures you emotionally. (Be patient, it takes some luck for that kind of novel to rise to the top, but it happens. How about Anne Tyler? Jane Hamilton? Meg Wolitzer? Kent Haruf? Tony Earley? Richard Russo?) Maybe you love the way an author integrates history into the story, or sets the protagonist in a sprawling family. You could do those things—about your subject, with your own sensibility. *Story is the key*.

If plotting is hard for you, pick a fairly short novel with a straightforward chronology, and take it apart. Think like an architect. Study archetypal plots, the plots of classic novels; practice by inventing your own versions in summary form. Then look at your summaries and find a way to upend the archetype. Look around you and keep asking questions—*What if? What else?*—because the best stories aren't labored; they spring from basic human needs and fears made new by imagination.

If your stories are thin, be more of the world. If you read a lot of fiction, read science, geography, politics, poetry, history. (I ignore current events in this regard—a matter of taste. I like for things to have settled a bit.) The annual "Best Of" collections are a great place to start. Believe me when I tell you those topics are full of stories. Some novelists gain fame by writing about characters in a certain field like art (Susan Vreeland) or science (Andrea Barrett). Readers love to learn something from a story, whether it's the history of the opium wars (Amitav Ghosh's Ibis trilogy), how to cook with truffles (Martin Walker's novels of the Dordogne), or how crimes are investigated.

Read translated work; it will expand your view of how stories are told and what matters. (Start with Nobel winners like Patrick Modiano, Mo Yan, Naguib Mahfouz, Halldór Laxness.) Travel, not just afar, but in your own home area with curiosity and appreciation. Join groups. Learn a new skill. See fewer popular movies. (They seed your mind with formulas.) Keep a journal. Ideas skitter. If you write them down, they accrue and cohere; they become something bigger, something else. Fodder. I once led a weekly workshop in which writers *told* stories. They could tell old tales, family stories, or things they made up. It's great practice—and fun—for writers, and for anyone.

Learn to think of stories as multidimensional. You learn about something someone did or something that happened to a family. Ask yourself: Who else had a story in that event? What was going on around the event? What stories intersect? You might find a fresh subject for a novel. (Consider Paula McLain's *The Paris Wife*, about Hemingway's first wife.)

Don't try to get on bandwagons. You can learn a lot by studying admirable novels—about structure, about developing characters, about integrating history into fiction, and so on. But trying to write a story like one that made another writer famous is a prescription for frustration. Fiction in young adult literature does seem to follow trends for a while, but (a) who came up with the first one?—that's the writer you want to be; and (b) nobody wants to be the last one who wore out the genre twist. Of course, if you can find a fresh interpretation for an old genre, go for it. *Gone Girl* made gothic thriller new again and has been madly recycled.

Go inside yourself. Every character you write has something of you in him. Don't stay on your own surface. Learn more about what fascinates you. Find the story in you and you will find the subjects for your novels. Fear, anger, shame, joy, ambition, pride, envy, loss, grief; what you need and don't have; what you had and lost; where you were and can't go back. Great themes are about ordinary human wants in extraordinary circumstances. Or the other way around. Flaubert set himself the challenge of writing a novel about an unsympathetic protagonist—a whiny, self-centered, grasping woman with no real redeeming qualities. Huh? He wanted the reader to understand her so completely that it would be impossible not to care about her. That's *Madame Bovary*. Some writers build their careers by being skillful at making every novel different, others by making their novels familiar. The simple truth is you have to find out where your passion takes you, something you care about so deeply you cannot help but find the right story and the right way to tell it.

Read what you love. Write from passion.

Exercises

Make a stack of novels you admire. Don't deliberate too much; choose them intuitively, by your feel for them. For each one, identify two features you admire. Consider how you can strive to have those qualities in your novel, too.

The idea is to identify qualities you might aspire to, and to consider how those qualities are related to the concepts you think about as you read this book. You can set goals for yourself. Maybe you won't write a novel like the one you chose, but if you liked the way it looked on the pages—the length of the chapters, for example—that tells you something to consider in planning your own structure. If you liked the friendly, informal tone of the diction, you can feel free to write in your natural voice, too. If the setting was evocative, you can remember that you want to think about creating a memorable setting.

If you love the way a first-person or close-third-person protagonist comments on her life and other people's behavior, saying things to the reader that made you laugh and shake your head—*You bet!*—then you might want to try incorporating more of your character's interiority into your own story. Or you may want to find opportunities for her to express her ideas to another character. Or you, too, can write in first person.

Perhaps what you love is the quickness of the read, the way the story flows with little adornment but a lot of movement. Look at a few pages from your manuscript and see if you can pare them down to make the pace faster.

You love the language itself, the beauty of the descriptions and the surprise of arrival at the end of a passage. So study sentences for a while, to improve the variety and quality of your own. (See recommended books in Resources.)

You like a novel that is multigenerational. Maybe instead of pulling in some backstory about your protagonist's mother and grandmother, should you build their stories and their voices into the plot?

You like a novel that is built almost entirely of scenes. Study at least four *consecutive* chapters and note several things: First, how much time elapses between chapters? Next, is any narrative summary used in transitions, or does the author go directly into the scene in each chapter? And finally, briefly describe the tone or mood of each chapter—how much variety is there across the four scenes?

A Review of
Narrative Elements

I HAVE FOUND that the first thing writers facing revision need is a way to talk about their text to themselves. If they get caught in the spiderweb stickiness of sentences right away, they'll never understand what they have failed to dramatize. They'll never learn to see wholes instead of parts—chapters instead of pages; scenes instead of sentences. If you don't want to start a revision by fixing word choices, what do you start on?

Certainly you must first weigh the heft of your story: Is it what you hoped for? Is it passionate? Wise? Funny? If you are excited and confident about the story itself, there are craft issues to tackle. You revise by analyzing things like setups and predictions and transitions; through lines ("threads") and pacing. You want to appraise whether you have "covered" aspects of story with a proper balance of "show" (scene) and "tell" (summary). I suggest that you start by describing what's there. Your job in revising is to make sure that what the reader reads is the story you wanted to tell. Also, when you describe a page or passage or chapter, you start to see where you are losing the thread or oozing instead of structuring scenes. I daresay tangled narrative elements are the major characteristic of unsuccessful novel drafts.

And the failure to be clear about what the narrative is doing on a particular page usually springs from not having a vocabulary to describe it.

It's helpful to think of narrative as a construction, with parts. This is not to say that all parts are, or should be, equal; nor to say that there is a perfect pattern. Different writers use narrative in different ways. Some like to build broad sweeps of story that cover a lot of time, and such novels require a different strategy from those that engage the reader in a chain of scenes over a shorter time span. The balance of show and tell varies. Likewise, writers differ in how much they reveal their characters' thinking; in how much they have to say about the world of the story, and how much they use a narrator's—an authorial—voice. All of these choices influence the shape of the story, its density (a perceived quality in books with a lot of narrative summary and commentary), and the story's voice.

I take a kind of Lego block approach to narrative structure. What I call a component could be a red block, or a yellow block, and so on. Your structure has more blue than mine; mine has more green. We have different ways of telling stories, and that difference is conveyed in the proportions of narrative elements we create.

These are the structural components I will discuss, and they will figure in your analysis of your manuscript, and in your plans for revision:

Scene
Scene summary and sequence
Scene fragments
Narrative summary
Exposition
Interiority: Response, reflection, interrogation, time, and
    commentary
Exposition versus interiority

A novel uses all of these elements, but from one book to another, the balance of them varies according to the authors' styles and choices and the needs of the story. I've written books that are essentially all scenes (*Opal on Dry Ground*; *More Than Allies*) and others that are dominated by summary and introspection (*Gringa*, *Walking Dunes*, *Plain Seeing*). I developed *Beyond Deserving* as a sequence of chapters, each with a key scene that I "nested" in exposition, summary, and interiority. Different stories require different narrative strategies. Compare Cormac McCarthy's *All the Pretty Horses* (it's all in the action) to Ian McEwan's *Atonement* or Michael Ondaatje's *The English Patient* (it's all in the telling). I think that the latter approach is more difficult to control, but a story, like a heart, wants what it wants, and the novel has the capacity for deep psychological archeology and sustained empathy with a character. It isn't that there is a right or a wrong proportion; rather, if you can be aware of your choices and evaluate them, you will be better able to create a strong framework that can hold the scope and tone of the story in the best way. You will find it easier to parse structural problems in a draft and to design a stronger revision. You will be able to revise deliberately, a different process from that of the draft, which can feel like a journey with little light.

You almost surely have a natural inclination toward structure and voice, and you can assess whether your default mode is best for you, or whether you want to try other approaches. Many writers do have a default mode that works well for them. I liked using very different structures for my novels.

Note that in the Resources section, where I talk about particular novels, I point out the way the authors use narrative structure, that is, whether they emphasize scenes or summaries, and so on. If you choose a particular novel for close study, do it with colored markers, pens and pencils, and the curiosity of a puzzle lover. Buy a used copy and cut it apart; make charts. Work to visualize the way stories are put together; your mind can hold schemas better if they have shape as well as words. You will soon recognize these elements easily, and as you study how other writers use them, you will become more conscious of and at ease with the choices you make. *Pay special attention to the transitions between scene and commentary.* Becoming deliberate in craft brings with it the occasional agony of self-consciousness—*Did I really do that?* and *What do I do now?*—but in time your skill becomes integral to your writing, something you tap automatically as you write and then exploit consciously when you identify problems in your text. Isn't that the way of building and using skills? Sometimes you play a game of tennis; sometimes you practice your backhand. Sometimes you play scales; sometimes a sonata.

Once you can automatically identify which narrative element you are reviewing, you can evaluate its function and its success. You can build smoother transitions. You can build stronger scene sequences. You can use the wonderful capacity of the novel to explore human consciousness.

NARRATIVE IS THE telling of events in a logical order. We are interested in those events that have consequences for characters.

Now let's look at its parts.

In conceiving of a novel, the most important thing is to have a strong story. I'm thinking of Story with a capital *S*: the idea that is large and deep enough to hold a book-length narrative. "Thin" stories are doomed. Some I have seen many times: Breakup stories. Rivalry in a family stories. Bang-bang crime stories. In other words, stories in which there's really only one main event, one layer.

You may not really know what the story is when you begin writing. If you make an outline, you'll capture some of the plot (the sequence of action), but you probably won't really understand your story until you explore it in writing. It's both the *what* of the book and the *why*.

Think about the difference between *complication* and *complexity*.

Complications are additions to the main line; tangles, if you will. More characters. More events. More questions. You have to have some, but you don't want to get lost in them. Farce has a lot of complications. Cozy novels tend to have them, too. *What? What?* the reader asks.

Complexity is about intricacy, about layers, depths. Events reverberate beyond the moments in which they occur. Characters carry their past, their desires, their inner conflicts, into the story. Tragedy, certainly, is about complexity, but so is any story with depth and resonance. *Why? Why?* the reader asks.

It's best to start with a unit of the story, so let's look at the scene; knowing how to write one is probably the most important skill a fiction writer needs, because drama is the heart of narrative. Even if the strategy of a novel emphasizes broad sweeps of summary rather than scene-by-scene development, the writer still has to convey the sense of things happening to characters, and characters making things happen and having feelings; there is in narrative always a dramatic current occurring in action displayed or implied. Everything that happens in real life happens in real time. In a novel, everything that happens to characters happens in the *idea* of real time, but you don't have enough pages to transcribe real time, so you choose when to enter it in a scene, and you summarize or imply the rest. One way or the other, you keep up momentum; there is always the sense of going forward (even when it involves looking back).

Scene

In a scene, characters do things and feel things. They act and react. If you want to test your scene, see if you can reduce it to a statement of what the event was (the thing that happened) and what the emotions were (what the character felt). Then ask yourself how the scene served the overall story.

In my novel *Walking Dunes*, there is a scene with this event:

David's mother—hungover, sloppy, and verbally abusive—stumbles into his room and discovers that he has a girl in his bed. Emotions: his embarrassment and anger. (Note: His mother is angry, too, but it's his scene.)

A scene has a function in the narrative. It has a reason for being there. It may introduce new plot elements or set up a situation for what is coming; it may show us the character's behavior so that we have a deeper understanding of her. The question you always have to ask is: Does this need to be a scene? (Could it be summarized instead? Could it be left out?) The scene with David and his mother exacerbates the teenager's feelings of dislocation in his parents' life, and subtly changes the tenor of his relationship with the girl. It also sets up the next scene, in which David's father storms in to castigate his son. Both scenes need to be dramatized so that the reader experiences the awful awkwardness of the situation (the girl in David's bed) and the quality of the relationships (son and mother, son and father), best conveyed in dialogue and gesture.

A scene has a kind of engine, something I call a "pulse." It is the energy that drives the scene. It is a current that runs beneath it. It is emotional—a state of desire or need, of passion. If the pulse is weak, the scene is weak. Even if the action is dramatic, it may be hollow. The pulse is why the scene matters. You can see why a scene written mostly to provide information, to get from one plot point to another, without an urgency of its own, can slow down the narrative and bore the reader. The writer has to engage the reader; a scene creates a little movie in the reader's head. And the blue ribbon goes to the scene that pierces the reader's heart.

A scene has a structure. It is a mini story. At its beginning, there is a situation, and at the end, there is a different one. Something has changed because of what happened. What I often see in apprentice writing is that the narrative slides into a scene. You find yourself in the scene but you're not oriented. *Huh?* is your reaction. *Weren't you just talking about something else?* There should be a clear beginning of or transition into a scene. The failure to establish the switch happens frequently when the author is describing a character's feelings and memories, and then all of a sudden the character is engaged with someone else, but it isn't clear how or why the shift occurred. If you are done with the subject that has been presented, check to see that the last sentence before the new scene feels finished. If the scene interrupts what comes before it, make sure you have a reason for why action is breaking into the thought. The point is to be deliberate and in control, not accidental and random. Sometimes the shift to a new paragraph signals the entry into a scene. The best situation is when the two passages, the non-scene and the scene that follows it, are thematically connected.

Likewise, there should be a rounding off at the end, perhaps into reflection or commentary, or, sometimes, a sudden break in the action. I ask my students to block out their scenes with colored markers. What we often see is that the scene doesn't start or end clearly. It is divided up by other aspects of narrative in ways that interrupt rather than cohere. It is diluted by lack of a clear structure.

Watching a movie can be a helpful way to practice this—I suggest that the movie be an indie or a foreign film. There isn't any way to muddle when a scene starts and ends because it's right there in front of you. You know when there is an end, a shift, a beginning. You want that same kind of clarity in your writing. Try watching part of a film sometime: Start a scene, watch a little bit, then go back to just before the scene began. Write a brief summary of what is happening before the scene you have chosen. It might be a panoramic sweeping view of countryside, or a rattling train ride, or a view of a rain-slick street. It might be a scene, but not the next one you are going to describe. Now run the film into the scene and describe what happens. Write it out in summary. Change video into prose. Indicate what the *first step of the scene* is. Do the same thing when the scene ends, that is, when there is a change to a different time or place. In a movie, nobody is talking about a scene; a scene just *is*. You know when you've left it *because you're not in it anymore*. You can see that on the screen. Well, you need to "see that" on the page, too.

Look at a published novel. Choose a scene and find exactly where it begins and exactly where it ends. Look at what came before and what came after. Do this exercise many times, with short scenes, long scenes, and scene fragments; and you'll understand what it means to keep the reader oriented with effective shifts in narrative.

Here is a brief excerpt from the novel *Evergreen* by Rebecca Rasmussen that illustrates what I am saying. The structure of the beginning of chapter 3 is this: **NS** (narrative summary); **SS** (short scene); **C** (commentary—a shift of subject).

NS Eveline spent the winter of her pregnancy reading Emil's taxidermy manuals, the only bound pages for mile after boundless mile. Of everything she packed that hurried September morning in Yellow Falls, books weren't something she'd considered stuffing into her suitcase, which meant she was stuck reading about dead animals now.

SS "Soon you'll be able to preserve me," Emil said when he came in from chopping wood on the first big snow day—two feet!—in November. He was growing a beard, which collected snow when he was chopping wood and, along with his foggy safety glasses, made him look a little like an owl until the snow melted.

"Just birds," Eveline said, even though she'd been secretly drawing pictures of babies when she was certain Emil was deep in the woods.

C No woman in Yellow Falls, and probably anywhere, talked about what it felt like to be pregnant other than to say it was the Lord's miracle, so Eveline didn't know to expect the cramping and expanding, the tenderness of her breasts and hips.

Of course scenes vary in length (as they vary in importance), and sometimes there is the need for only a moment of a scene, and it can be embedded in summary. But I strongly assert that you should know which strategy you are using: full ("kernel," or "major") scene, little ("minor") scene, or scene fragment. And the most important scenes in a novel, what I later discuss as "core scenes," should function with the integrity of small stories. Get your colored markers and find your scene blocks. They are the lifeblood of your story.

EXERCISES

For each of the suggestions, turn to your manuscript and ask if you have accomplished them. Look at one of your major scenes right now.

Think of scenes as mini stories.

❏ If it is a mini story, you will be able to identify the beginning, middle, and end. Mark your scene into three blocks of text. Your scene will have a resolution that leaves things different from how they were when the scene began. Write a statement about the beginning that says "how it was," and another about the end that says "how it is now." Are they truly different? Did the scene really make that difference? Did something happen?

Write scenes about moments that matter.

❏ If the scene is important enough to take up space in the novel, what happens in it *matters*. What is the particular "something that matters" in your scene? State it in a sentence. Why does it matter? In the excerpt above from *Evergreen*, the scene seems uneventful, but it is early in the story, and the young woman is just learning what she has got herself into in the wilderness. She's just learning who her husband is in this new setting, and what being pregnant means. Those few lines tell us a lot about the situation and the relationship of the characters. They may be in love, but they aren't entirely comfortable with one another; there's a lot to learn about living together.

Know the boundaries of your scene.

❏ If your scene stands alone (i.e., it is not immediately followed by another scene), you can put your finger on the line where it begins, and then on the line where it ends. Everything between is the scene: action, response. Draw heavy double lines at the beginning and end of the scene; now underline the sentence that comes before the scene starts, and the one that comes after the scene ends. Those are your transition sentences. (You may have made a "jump" into the scene after white space—a different strategy.) The scene may be "nested" in exposition or commentary, but it has its own structure. Employ parts of scenes—compressions, fragments—in summaries and transitions.

❏ If one scene follows another, identify the way that you have bridged the story between scenes, especially if time has passed between them. There's a good chance you used (or should use) summary as your transition. If you need to review the two sections on summary, which follow, you can come back to this exercise later. The sections are "Scene summary" and "Narrative summary."

Scene summary and scene sequence

If there is a lot of action in your novel, especially if it covers a broad scope of time, you won't be able to develop all of it in scenes. Yet there will be places where you are reluctant to let go of scene elements: the feeling for setting, moments of action or emotion, something to allow an economical flow of story while also creating the sense of having participated in an event. Often, you want a sequence of scenes, one thing happening after another, but you don't want all of them to take the same space on the page. You want variety and emphasis in scenes, just as you do in sentences, and of course you don't want unnecessary length. *You can link scenes in a sequence by summarizing some of them.* It's like stringing a necklace with some large stones and some small ones.

It is possible to convey a scene in a compressed fashion, not taking the time to develop all the moments in the event (the "beats," or steps of action), but telling enough that the reader could describe the scene himself, from his imagination. *The scene is there, behind the summary.* The reader could stop and imagine a filled-out version, but he doesn't have to, because you have given him the *sense of what happened and how it felt.* If the summarized scene is part of a sequence, this keeps the movement of actions connected, while allowing for the greater accent on the more important ones. Dialogue is mostly reduced to indirect discourse. (So instead of writing, *He said, "I can't go right now,"* you write, *He said he couldn't go.*) The key is for the scene summary in a sequence, like the scene, to cover a short period of time. It is about something contained enough that you could have written it as a full scene, with details about setting and movements, but you decided that you couldn't devote the space to it, or you wanted to present it as an auxiliary to a more important scene. *In a novel, you are always balancing economy and elaboration, plot and character, meaning and action.*

Here is an example from *Walking Dunes:*

They ate in the dining room, served by a maid. He said thank you when she ladled soup into his bowl, but the Kimbroughs did not acknowledge the service, and he decided to do only what he first observed. He ate lightly, for him, out of self-consciousness. There were certain obligatory questions about his family, which he answered with a briskly polite brevity. His father was a tailor, his mother a nurse. There was the sister, married to a "radio executive." The answers seemed to satisfy; he was not required to elaborate. There was of course no way for him to ask the things he wanted to know, details about Hayden's role on the bank board, the nature of his law practice. It was like dining with Africans and never mentioning the home country; not having traveled, he did not know enough to formulate inquiry. Beth and her mother moved their food around on their plates, eating little, and though the maid said there was a cobbler, they declined dessert. Hayden said, wouldn't that make a good snack later? and David of course claimed to be altogether too satisfied with the meal to have another bite.

This passage is followed by another scene summary, moving David through his first visit to his girlfriend's home, establishing his sense of awkwardness, a poor boy out of place in the company of the rich. Many chapters in the novel are developed in this way: A scene sequence presents events that accrue, allied in time, moving the protagonist on his trajectory from a promising but poor high school boy to a young man facing moral decisions he may not have the wisdom or strength of character to manage.

Exercises

❏ Choose a scene from a novel you know—the scene should be at least a page and a half long, but not much longer—and then compress it to a half page of manuscript. (You are looking at a published book, then producing around 150 words.) You want to tell what happened without all the details. When you feel comfortable doing this, go to a longer scene; your summary will also be longer, about a

page. (Repeat this exercise to get good at summarizing. I
have my students do it dozens of times.)

❑ Now browse through a chapter and see if you can identify
short passages that summarize action as a way to get from
one scene to another when the second scene doesn't follow
immediately in time. You know you are reading summary
if you can imagine expanding the text to a longer passage
with more details.

Scene fragments

One of the most common ways scene fragments are used is
when a character reflects about something that happened in the
past, and a flash of memory is called up. It's a little like looking
at a snapshot that captures a moment of time in something that
was ongoing. In my novel *Plain Seeing*, the protagonist, Lucy, is
remembering what it has been like since she had a bad accident.
(She was struck by a car while walking across an intersection.)
She "had been as helpless as a torn bag for weeks." The ordeal
of the accident and of the care that has been required are described in summary, and then there is this short paragraph:

In the ambulance, she had seen Andy. His camera was
swinging from his neck; she looked straight into the
uncapped lens. "It's my fault," she remembered hearing
him say.

Note the detail about Andy's camera—the stuff of a scene—
and of course the dialogue. Then Lucy's memories return in
summary to memories further in the past, when, if she had not
made regrettable mistakes, her life could have taken a different
turn. One of the ways that a scene fragment works well is for it
to be taken from a full scene that occurred earlier, or for it to
expand an earlier scene in some way. In this case, Lucy's accident was described in a previous chapter, but the fragment pre-

sented here adds to the event in the later moment when she sees her lover. When the scene was happening, this moment wasn't significant. Now, looking back, it is.

Sometimes a novel will have a memory that is so important that it comes up again and again, each time calling up an image that becomes an echo, or what I call a "ghost," because it is like a hovering memory. The effect should be to touch the reader emotionally by reminding her, as the character is reminded, of the prior dramatic event. The trick is to not take a dramatic moment and beat it to death, a fairly common ploy in sloppy popular fiction.

Scene fragments are usually embedded in narrative summary or in character interiority. Sometimes they recur like the ghosts I just spoke of, when a character least expects them, casting a shadow over the present event. The reader may not even realize how significant they are, and how much they are affecting her feelings as she reads.

Narrative summary

I know I said writing a scene is the most important skill, but now I must say summary is undervalued. The word sounds so perfunctory, as if one is writing something to get it out of the way. But summary simply means compression, as paper is made from pulp. All the grit is pressed out, and we are left with the flow of story, transporting the reader through time (a day, a week, a year) in a way that conveys the drama of events and sets up the readiness and the hunger for the next passage that enters the story scenically. Information (exposition) is relayed so that what follows will have context. Writers of historical fiction, of pageantry, of sagas, have to be very good at this. I think of Amitav Ghosh, Dickens, Edward Rutherfurd, Rohinton Mistry's *A Fine Balance*, Yaa Gyasi's *Homegoing*, Ken Follett's *The Pillars of the Earth*, Paulette Jiles's *News of the World*. But any book-length work of fiction sometimes needs to move things along economically, and besides, the well-written summary can be a beautiful piece of prose indeed. Jim Harrison used big chunks of narrative summary to push time forward in his novels. Summary has a sense of movement and a rhythm and a long view, and those things are pleasurable. When you catch yourself as you are reading a novel, stopping to read a passage again, I bet it is often because you have just read a beautifully composed narrative summary and have been caught up in its cadence and imagery. I hasten to emphasize that summary works when it is deliberate, designed, composed, and polished. It shouldn't be strung through in broken segments at points when the writer happened to remember something the reader needs to know.

As I mentioned earlier, in *Walking Dunes* I used narrative summary as a major structural strategy. Chapters cover whole swaths of time. Chapter 3 covers an entire summer of David's life, just prior to the events in the "now" of the novel. It begins like this:

David Puckett had lived much of that summer of 1958 in an old beauty parlor in Fort Stockton. His father had rented the building as a store for the third year in a row, but this time he hired his son to spend half of each summer month there alone, doing business with the local people, both Anglo and Mexican. David sold yard goods (mill ends and damaged fabrics), clothing (discontinued or imperfect), and some Army surplus goods. Four or five days a month he traveled to outlying towns like Iraan and Rankin, sleeping at night in the station wagon and setting up sales tables wherever he could. He liked being out from under his father's eye. He liked feeling he was on his own. And he told himself, as his father had told him, that he was doing a service to these communities, selling cheap goods nobody else wanted to people who needed them, for bargain prices they could barely afford.

The function of this chapter is to give the reader a portrait of the boy at the point where he becomes a young man, faced with choices about what kind of person he wants to be and what kind of life he wants to live. It begins by talking about his summer work, but one of the things that characterized that summer for him was that, being so much alone, he became deeply introspective. He thought about who he was and how he had become himself. So the chapter soon continues:

> He had been listing the events of his life. It was merely a way to combat boredom. He had thought of the list as an inventory, and he had been amazed at the ways he could vary it. It gave him an odd sense of power to realize that what he left off and what he put on the list changed the quality of his history.

So he thinks about childhood illnesses and family history, about school and the books he loved. He thinks of his parents as characters with fascinating stories—he sees that their marriage has turned bitter, and that his home life is stagnant, sloppy, pathological. How he envies the lives of ordinary families!

David has been much influenced by a favorite teacher and the literature she had him read, especially Fitzgerald and Hardy. He has a kind of writerly mind, seeing the story in real events, wondering about meaning, admiring writers for the "largeness of their visions." The chapter tells about a girl he meets during that summer, and about what she might have meant to him. His deep introspection is intelligent but naive, a good description of who he is. All of this history and information (exposition and reflection and interrogation) could be conveyed only through summary, but the summary leaves the reader with a good idea of what David's life has been like and how he got to the place he is at age eighteen, in his senior year of high school.

Scene summaries like this are often—get ready—embedded in a dramatic scene, part of the laying out of history and character.

In other words, interrupting the ongoing action. This architecture is something the novel can embrace—the reader can embrace—as long as the interrupting summary is tied to the dramatic scene and there is clarity for the reader regarding just which scene she is reading. If a character is remembering something and going over her feelings about it while she is walking through a park, for example, you could insert a line or two that places her in that setting, perhaps something that catches her attention, and then go back to her thoughts. This is exactly the strategy used by Dominic Smith in *The Last Painting of Sara de Vos* when he portrays the protagonist walking Manhattan's streets, brooding about the theft of his painting and his obsession with finding the person who has kept the painting *and* forged it. For him to think while he is walking specific streets grounds the character. It keeps the reader's interest. What apprentice novelists often do instead is simply to introduce a kind of free-floating cloud of feelings and thoughts, without establishing that the character is in a physical setting. Worse, this often happens in a way that interrupts or muddily ends a scene that had a different purpose and action. On the other hand, an experienced writer (or just a careful one) can "stop action" for thought, if the transition into and out of the musing is carefully handled.

I want to emphasize that *you must know what you are doing when you interrupt a scene*. If you are deliberate about it (perhaps in revision), it's much more likely to accomplish what you hoped for.

The parts of narrative that seem to "meander" must have a clear purpose, like one of these:

1. To illuminate what has happened.
2. To prepare the reader for what is coming.
3. To cover events economically so that there is a "past" to the present of the novel.
4. To show the character engaged in conflicted feelings.

Many novels are written with more narrative summary and scene summary than outright scenes; sometimes the scene is the "interruption" in the flow of narrative, rather than the other way around. It's a matter of style and also of the story. Jim Harrison was a master summarizer. Reading him, I would sometimes realize that the action I'd been reading—and had been engrossed in—wasn't developed in scenes. His scenes, unsurprisingly, are dense and taut, too; the main difference between his summary and scene is how much time is covered.

If your natural instinct is to write in summary, to muse, to describe, I urge you to know the novel's sequence of major scenes as clearly as stepping-stones across an expanse of garden, and to weigh the distance and the "stuff" that comes between them so that you keep the reader aware of the forward movement of story, even when he is enjoying the deep ruminations of character or narrator. *The Good Mother*, by Sue Miller, is an example of a book with a lot of commentary and summary that never loses sight of what is happening, so the novel's tension doesn't go lax. One of my favorite writers of what I call "intellectually elaborated scenes" is Mavis Gallant, whose long stories have the heft of novellas.

The roaming narrative can enrich and deepen the experience of a novel, and for me, a novel without it is shallow. But if you find it difficult to control the progress of scenes nested in expansive commentary, I suggest you strengthen the scene sequences first. That's where the drama is.

EXERCISES

❏ Think of something that happened to you on one day in your life. It can be a big or small event: You bought your first car. You proposed to your future wife. You had a fender bender. You moved out of a house.

Now tell what happened in no more than fifty words. That is narrative summary.

❑ Find a passage in your manuscript that summarizes an event or the progress of events across time without elaborating in scenes.

First, identify what the summary contributes to your story. Is it concerned with the past or what is happening now? Does it help the reader understand what is happening at this point in the novel?

Next, identify what comes right before and right after the passage of summary. In other words, describe your structure. Is it nested in a scene, or does it come between scenes? When you read into and out of the summary, do you think the reader will follow the flow without being confused?

Exposition

Exposition presents information such as history, setting, family structure, and so on. It describes a farmhouse, a brother's envy, a war's progression, the great blizzard of 1967. It may be what happened in the past, or the way things are now, but it is information necessary to fully understand the events of the novel or the context in which events occurred, while it is not narratively necessary to "show" it in dramatic text.

Everything I said about inserting scene summaries applies to exposition, too: It can enrich your narrative, if it adds to what it is interrupting, and if you give clear cues to the reader as you go in and out of the foreground scene.

Interiority: Response, reflection, interrogation, and commentary

The next three elements of narrative structure center on what we can call the character's "interiority," that is, internal thoughts.

Response is the emotional reaction of a character, and sometimes the character's urge to action. It might be a sudden swell of tears or a march across the room. It might be a stiffening wave of humiliation that makes her refuse to look at anyone. It follows action.

Apprentice writers often have a default sense of response that consists of alternating a character's remarks, or some other expression of her feelings, with sentences that describe what is going on in the scene. It gets tedious very fast.

Reflection is the more studied response, a time of considering and weighing aspects of one's experience. It may result in a new resolve, or an impulse toward forgiveness. It may mire the character in hopeless anguish, or cause her to see things in a way that interprets the behavior of others. It isn't "in the moment" the way response is. It's not holy or necessarily intellectual; it can be as wrongheaded as any other aspect of character behavior, but it does involve a little time spent thinking.

Reflection could interrupt a flow of action, but usually this isn't a good idea; we are more likely to see it work at the close of a scene, or at a later time when the character has time alone.

Interrogation is that part of reflection that asks questions about what has happened: the *whys* that nettle a person. Sometimes it means looking deeply into oneself, taking or shirking responsibility for life's turns. It might be focused on what lies ahead and what one should do about it, resulting in resolution. It may raise the question *What is the right thing to do?* and thus introduce conflicted thinking. It creates tension. This is the kind of interiority that lets the reader understand who a character really is, what she cares about, what is driving her.

I will talk about interiority more later, but I want to make the point that the three types just described can each be used in three different time-sensitive reactions to ongoing events in the story.

Something happens and the character thinks about it from one of these three perspectives:

1. Something that happened before.
2. Something that is going on right now.
3. Something that might happen in the future.

Here is an example of interiority from my novel *Plain Seeing*. The protagonist, Lucy, marries a young man she meets in graduate school. The first chapter to introduce their relationship has several passages of narrative summary, to get them from their first meeting toward the heart of their story—the dissolution of their marriage fifteen years later. Essentially, the chapter comprises chunks of time in their early relationship.

In the passage below, there is an implied scene, but the function of the passage is to show Lucy's changes in consciousness across time. Thus the interiority is response and reflection, based on what has happened up to the implied scene. The scene in this case is secondary to the interiority! Notice the scene fragments, which pick up the thread introduced by the first sentence of the passage. I have underlined the fragments. The scene conveys Lucy's emotional leap from self-pity to guarded optimism about her life. It has a "sweep" to it that is larger than a single scene. It has the sound of something in the past looked at from a later, wiser perspective. Note, too, that the text is an observation of Lucy's thinking, rather than the sound of her voice.

<u>The first time Lucy slept with Gordon, she cried.</u> It was surprising and embarrassing and wonderful to discover so much feeling. She had thought there was only pain, that it lasted forever, that she couldn't give in or show it to anyone. Sex and lacrimation had never occurred together before. She had thought of herself as brave and sporty, picking partners who thought they had picked her. Her tears had been childhood tears, hot and sullen and secretive. She had cried out of resentment and impatience, but never for joy. <u>Then she lay beneath him and tears washed out of her eyes, down her temples into her hair and onto the pillow. Her chest heaved.</u>

There were things she wanted to tell him—to tell someone—but she swallowed the words, to be the woman he might love. She was twenty-one years old. She thought she was very grown up. She had put herself through college. This was in 1964, in Austin, Texas. Jackie was a widow. (At least those children had a mother!) Lyndon was President. She was in her first semester of graduate school, not looking very far ahead.

<u>He smoothed her hair back and shushed her again and again.</u>

<u>He thought it was something he had done. "I'm sorry, I'm sorry," he said. She put her fingers to his lips.</u> She couldn't stop crying. There were many tears inside, capped, like a well. He had opened a valve in her with his courtly, gentle manner, his sweet shyness that turned ardent, then encompassing.

She knew nothing of the manners of his class. She had never been with a man before who didn't forget all about her at his climax. Gordon was a scholar. By day, he was all decorum. She believed that something about her had ignited him, and the thought thrilled her, then made her cry.

<u>When she could talk, she whispered, "I come with nothing, a motherless child."</u> She assumed fatherless was implied. She knew as soon as she said it that she was breaking his heart—he carried photographs of his parents in his wallet—that he would marry her, that she would never have to be alone again. Her sorrow, her burden, her empty heart were suddenly of value, the coin of a new kingdom. She needed him, and her need was her gift to him, her dowry. She felt powerful, as if she were beautiful. She understood, for the moment, the pleasure of power and beauty. She felt like her mother, only luckier.

Commentary, as I use the word, means the ways that the author finds to "say something about life": about psychology and philosophy, faith, fate, and doubt; about what has happened; about God and country, race and sex and love and grief—all those good things.

It is very tricky to do this well, because it requires deft handling of point of view (POV). American fiction has been dominated by the close-third-person voice for decades, which little allows the long view of commentary, but sometimes a clever author will skirt the limitations of third person by having the character think the things the writer wants said. *Adroit handling of point of view is essential to commentary*. It is usually easier to write a "novel of commentary" with a first-person narrator, but third-person POV can allow a kind of immediacy in commentary very much like first person.

Again, the best way to understand this is to read a chapter in a novel and look for it. Some novels are full of commentary—there should be a name for the type. Done well, such books are marvels of story and thought. Think of Doris Lessing, J. M. Coetzee, Julian Barnes, Saul Bellow, Philip Roth, Kate Atkinson, Francine Prose. Think of *Middlemarch*!

And there are lively contemporary novels like Meg Mitchell Moore's *The Arrivals*, in which family members—grown kids come home, with their kids—endlessly consider their own lives and relationships. The interiority is a mix of all types: memories, resentments, hopes for change, observations about marriage and motherhood, and most of all, about how life doesn't turn out the way you think it is going to. Here is a snippet. Lillian is sitting on a bench with her little girl, Olivia.

Lillian patted the spot beside her on the bench. She closed her eyes. Perhaps Olivia could be persuaded to fall asleep in the sun with her. She was trying to convince herself—and the Popsicles were part of this ploy—that this was merely a vacation, just a little jaunt to visit the family, and that at some point soon they would return home and resume their normal existence. She had found that by keeping her marital wound tightly covered, indeed, by refusing to acknowledge it at all, and by refusing to acknowledge the now rudderless state that accompanied it, it hurt much less.

In Nancy Clark's comedy of manners, *The Hills at Home*, again an extended family is packed into a single house. Point of view and opinions bounce around on every page like Ping-Pong balls: *Everyone* is commenting on *everyone's* behavior all the time! Both books accomplish their multivocal soul-searching by throwing rules of point of view out the window; everyone has a voice. It makes me think maybe literary advice is just a cozy form of passing down old rules, right when dozens of writers are breaking them. You can, too, if you can make your novel work. More on this in the section on point of view.

You may have read *The Stranger* by Albert Camus in college. I recommend reading it again, attending to the way Camus deftly threads the protagonist Meursault's observations into the actions. (The POV is first person.) We think of the book being about a man disengaged from life, but in fact he is constantly commenting on life and his experience; it is in the moment when the sun strikes his eyes and he shoots the Arab that his consciousness fails him. Otherwise, the whole novel is a brilliant, beautifully paced accrual of awareness until Meursault's recognition of his fate, in the light of *what life is*, leads him to accept his impending death.

Here is an excerpt late in the book, after Meursault's trial:

I'd realized that the most important thing was to give the condemned man a chance. Even one in a thousand was good enough to set things right. So it seemed to me that you could come up with a mixture of chemicals that if ingested by the patient (that's the word I'd use: "patient") would kill him nine times out of ten. But he would know this—that would be the one condition. For by giving it some hard thought, by considering the whole thing calmly, I could see that the trouble with the guillotine was that you had no chance at all, absolutely none. The fact was that it had been decided once and for all that the patient was to die. It was an open-and-shut case, a fixed arrangement, a tacit agreement that there was no question of going back on. If by some extraordinary chance the blade failed, they would just start over. So the thing that bothered me most was that the condemned man had to hope the machine would work the first time. And I say that's wrong. And in a way I was right. But in another way I was forced to admit that that was the whole secret of good organization. In other words, the condemned man was forced into a kind of moral collaboration. It was in his interest that everything go off without a hitch.

In *The Great Gatsby* we have another first-person narrator, Nick Carraway, but he is more an observer of others, especially Gatsby, and at the book's close he functions as the voice of the story, that is, the author Fitzgerald, when he comments on the society he has been watching.

And as the moon rose higher the inessential houses began to melt away until gradually I became aware of the old island here that flowered once for Dutch sailors' eyes—a fresh, green breast of the new world. Its vanished trees, the trees that had made way for Gatsby's house, had once pandered in whispers to the last and greatest of all human dreams; for a transitory enchanted moment man must have held his breath in the presence of this continent, compelled into an aesthetic contemplation he neither understood nor desired, face to face for the last time in history with something commensurate to his capacity for wonder.

One of the most interesting things about Mark Haddon's novel *The Curious Incident of the Dog in the Night-Time* is the commentary of the narrator, the boy Christopher, who is autistic. He breaks the flow of action—usually going into a separate chapter—to explain his way of seeing things: why he doesn't "get" what other people are feeling, and why he doesn't much care, but also how he tries to understand people who are important to him; how he sees life as a set of puzzles to be solved, and how he is very good at math, where things are clearly puzzles and there's no overlay of sentiment and no one expects you to feel something. It was a daring thing to write, this novel, because the author had to make a character incapable of empathy sympathetic to the reader!

Exposition versus interiority

Exposition should be interesting in its own right, even as it amplifies prior or later action. It is always clarifying, never obfuscating. Its appearance should never so interrupt action that dramatic engagement is lost.

Interiority should deepen the engagement of reader with character. Its purpose is not primarily expository; it should not be necessary to the action, though it is usually triggered by action. It is enriching and emotional. When it explores a character's emotional conflict, it adds to dramatic tension. And it brings the reader into deep empathy.

The chapter about the teenage David cited earlier illustrated the narrative components we think of as "information" and "interiority." Exposition tells the reader about character or setting or past events in summary form, rather than trying to illustrate those things in scenes. In his rich saga *Sea of Poppies*, Amitav Ghosh tells about the voyage of a vast ship, the *Ibis*, just before the outbreak of the Opium Wars in China. He opens his novel with a long scene, but he soon shifts to exposition and conveys the history of the ship. This is necessary to the story, and it is fascinating. He doesn't plop it in the middle of a scene, breaking up a line of action and confusing the reader. He deftly treats his narrative components as building blocks, so that each kind of narrative accomplishes its purpose and then a shift occurs. As a reader, you don't think: Oh, that's exposition, that's summary, that's scene. But as a writer, you do, and when you analyze a novel and see how neatly the pieces fit together, you recognize the importance of pattern and plan. (Thus: Get out the colored pens. Turn a novel, or a section of one, into a visual lesson.)

One of the most common problems apprentice novelists have is the urgent impulse to explain everything to the reader. I think a lot of this is because the writer is figuring things out as he goes along, thinking on the page; it is perfectly understandable. In a first draft, this might be necessary, and being self-conscious about it could hamstring the story's development. In revision, though, the writer should be analytical and surgical. For example, a chapter may be centered on an important event, presented in scene, but the scene is interrupted with bits of information that make the scene feel disjointed and that disengage the reader. The revising writer has to ask: Does the reader need this information to understand this scene? If so, should I present it earlier? Should I follow the scene with summary or response, rather than inserting so much information within the scene?

Certainly it is possible to squeeze exposition into a scene deftly, but I suggest that you closely study writers you like, and specifically identify which parts of a long passage are scenic (dramatic) and which are expository. Use two colors of pen to underline the passages. Ask yourself: Why does the writer put this information here? Does the reader need it? How does the writer slip in and out of scene? How is the reader kept oriented and involved in the action? Consider, too, that a novelist will sometimes use a scene—say a man is chopping wood and stacking it—as a placeholder for extended interiority—say he is having an affair and he doesn't know how to break it off. The "scene" is more like a setting; it keeps the reader in touch with the character without really developing the tension and turn of a classic scene.

Ann Patchett is very good at writing novels full of intriguing information—and well-paced scenes. (See *State of Wonder*.)

Lots of old novels employ this strategy: *A Tree Grows in Brooklyn. Little Women.* "Big" novels like *Hawaii* and *Exodus.* Marge Piercy's robust multivoiced *Gone to Soldiers.* More recently, Rohinton Mistry's *A Fine Balance.* (Lots of Indian writers come out of the sweeping-canvas style of nineteenth-century Britain; their books are clotted with description and information. They write books you get lost in, books that take you weeks to read.) Exposition can be woven in quite economically, too, as in Kurt Palka's *The Piano Maker,* which teaches the reader a lot about the business and craft of making pianos, without ever slowing down the almost hypnotic engagement of the story.

You want to be deliberate about the way character thought is conveyed and where it is placed. Having a character think about and comment on every aspect of action in rotation is usually amateurish. To break the habit of alternating action with comment in a repetitive pattern, I encourage apprentice writers to practice writing scenes with no interiority at all. What people say and do ought to convey story in a scene. Yes, you want your characters to express emotions, too, but save the gnawing of the soul for the places where you are ready for the story to slow down, where the character is struggling with a decision, for example. Let your characters chew over something about which they are conflicted. Let them tussle with fear, jealousy, grief, ambition—emotions big enough to warrant space on the page. *Let your interiority raise and wrestle with questions.*

The Swedish mystery writer Mari Jungstedt (*Unspoken*) usually sticks to action in her scenes and then follows with an extended passage of response and resolve by the protagonist. I'm not suggesting that this is the best or only way to balance action and interiority, but it is instructive to try the pattern. It keeps the pace of the scene steady, and then moves into emotional reaction in a way that makes the response have a little arc of its own. It's schematic, but for a beginning novelist, it might be a calm, clear strategy for sorting out structure; you can always fiddle with passages again later to vary the pattern.

We'll deal with the challenge of using interiority well later on, but meanwhile, watch for it in your reading, and be conscious of it in your writing.

A note: You will already have noticed that I am asking you lots of questions and making suggestions for ways you can study novels to learn how they are put together. I'd like to think you would attend to every prompt, now or later. You might underline something you want to come back to, or make a note in the margin or in your journal. The more analysis you do, step by step, the more you will absorb the principles I am presenting to you. The exercises will help you master concepts. The easier the work will become. And the more you will accomplish.

EXERCISES

❏ Select one of your shorter scenes, a page or two. Go through it and underline all the sentences that convey action. Then double-underline the sentences that convey interiority (response, reflection, interrogation, commentary). (Alternatively, use two colors.)

Now write the scene out as all action and read it for its effect. You may find holes in the action, or the scene may be just fine. Consider each of the sentences of interiority and make a new decision about whether to include them (a) at all or (b) at the same place or (c) at the end of the scene.

Try more than one arrangement and see what you think of the new scene. Look at it on another day. Obviously this is an analysis you can perform for all scenes. It helps you confirm the line of action as well as the usefulness of interiority.

❏ Select a scene from a published book. Choose one that has a lot of interiority. Using the definitions from this chapter, catalog the kinds of interiority the author uses in the scene. Is the character's thinking focused on *right now*, or on the past or future? Does the interiority feel close to the action, or does the character link what is happening to other events or concerns?

An afterthought

Do successful novelists think about all the aspects of writing that I have raised? I can't say. I suppose there have been many storytellers from whom stories flowed much less self-consciously than I am suggesting here. Literature, like music, science, and the visual arts, has its geniuses, and I wouldn't dare to suppose how they produce their work. But I know that there are many fine essays about writing that indicate a deep level of analysis of process by gifted writers. (You could spend a nice month reading interviews in past issues of *The Paris Review*.) There are many letters among writers about the toil, thrill, and mystery of writing. Gustave Flaubert famously agonized over every detail of his writing and complained about it often. He once told George Sand that he worked to avoid assonance in his sentences. He wrote a friend that he was very weary of Mme. Bovary. (He spent five years writing that novel.) And Henry James, bless him, seems to have written down everything he ever thought about writing. We know he was always observing, always "taking notes," always questioning human behavior, always imagining how circumstances produce stories and, most of all, *how he was going to use what he was learning.*

Taking prose apart in order to identify and discuss its components doesn't mean that each type of text "stands alone" in a manuscript. Of course scenes will often have exposition and interiority and not just action. Of course summaries will have fragments of scenes. The more accomplished the writer, the more difficult it is to parse a text; elements are expertly interwoven. That said, I encourage you to identify the *major narrative structural component* you are working with at a particular time. If you know you are writing a dramatic scene, you know that action and tension are paramount. When you write exposition, you know to ask yourself: Is this where I need this? Does it interrupt the scene too much? Or does it add to the scene by creating understanding and context? When the character is thinking, you ask those same questions. And of course there is a reason for interiority: It enriches our understanding of a character; it fills in context; it reminds us of things that have already happened, and if it involves a conflict of intention or emotion, it creates tension. Knowing that, you have standards to which you hold your passages of a character thinking. You recognize when you are spinning too far away, or taking up too much page space from the ongoing drama. Always, always, your concern is to keep things moving.

If interiority is long-winded, it must enrich the reader's understanding and empathy. It must be pleasurable to read. It must occur when the narrative needs a break, at a place that slows the pace, or when the reader needs to understand a character's feelings. Sometimes interiority can be breathless, anxious, conflicted. Sometimes it is melancholy and measured. It reflects the events through the emotions and intellect of the character.

You should always be conscious of the temporal relationship of the thinking to the present action: Is the character looking back, looking forward (and building tension about what is coming), or deeply interrogating or responding to *this moment*.

Does the progression of thought fit?

Does it enhance the story?

Is it in balance with the overall function of the passage?

Am I carrying the reader along in the stream of story?

Exercise

❑ You will need pens of three colors to mark a passage.

Choose a novel that can serve you as a model. Find a passage or section of a chapter that is three to five pages long. Make a copy you can mark up.

Color 1: Block out *scenes*. Underline the sentences that are *action*.

Color 2: Block out *narrative summary or exposition*. Some may be in scenes.

Color 3: Double-underline *interiority*. This is likely to be in scenes, often at the end of a scene or, if set within a scene, entering and leaving it with sentences of transition.

Now describe the passage you have studied in terms of its *structure*.

What did you like about the way the author handled the balance of action and interiority?

II

Revision of a Novel Draft: Discussion and Exercises

Stages of Revision

THIS SCHEME WILL give you a way to think about your story with both a "long arc" and a "short arc." The whole manuscript adds up. That's the long view. The story can be talked about in terms of structure, plot, character, etc. Each of those perspectives is a short arc, and addressing them assists your overall ability to express the sum of your purpose and your craft.

You have to have a strong purpose in the second draft

This is the draft in which you understand the complexities of your story better and learn more about what you were trying to say all along. The primary goal is to strengthen the story.

If your first draft was too "thin," now you develop a greater robustness, whether it means rebuilding scenes, adding new action or subplots, or exploring character emotions more deeply.

You weed out what you now perceive to be extraneous.

You may decide to write a second draft before you begin the analytical work of revision. The key is to feel you have a story.

Walk and write

Early on in my writing, I got in the habit of telling myself my story while I took walks. The more times I told it, the more I learned about it. Most of the shifts were subtle, but sometimes I discovered a missing building block or an insight into a character. And when I say I told myself the story, I mean I talked aloud as I walked around my neighborhood. Back at my desk, I tried to tell the story in a page. When I felt I'd done okay at that, I wrote a longer summary—three or four pages. The story, condensed in this fashion, wasn't clogged by my problems with description or dialogue or scene structure; it didn't matter how I was going to fashion the chapters. What mattered was the story—what happens, to what consequence—and character, the protagonist whose deeds and fate are the heart of the novel. This work took a week or two, and after that, all the way through my revision, I wrote a one-page summary at least once a week, without looking at the old ones, usually after a walk. It made me feel grounded and in control. It freed me from one aspect of invention to focus on other aspects. It was like having a picture of a dress on the wall and a bolt of material on my table. I just had to make one from the other.

The scenario: A valuable tool

You know that in a scene you play out the narrative in dramatic action. In narrative summary, you compress scenes for economy's sake, or because the action isn't dramatic enough to merit the space. There is a difference in the level of detail. You can do the same thing as a planning tool, reducing text to its essence so that it can be part of a list or outline.

A scenario is an economical dramatic narration that is a functional summary of what happens in a story; it is a tool, not a product.

A scenario isn't written for style, it is written for narrative information. It serves a function similar to a study drawing for a painter. You can write a scenario that covers the whole narrative of the whole novel. You can write a scenario of a single scene. Ditto with a chapter. You can write a summary of a paragraph. In every case, it is easier to consider the story globally when you have compressed it. You also find a summary makes it easier to talk about your story in a writers' group. And you can write a guide to your revision in scenario form at different levels of detail. Think of the scenario as a reviser's basic brick.

Here is an excerpt of a scenario of *The Spoils of Poynton*, a novel by Henry James, which I found online at www.henryjames.org .uk/spoynt/, under "Story Synopses."

1st Level Synopsis (Summary)

Fleda Vetch, a principled but ultimately weak-willed young lady, becomes involved in a dispute between an antique collector and her son: he has inherited her collection on the death of her husband and wishes her to move out of the house but is planning to marry a girl she views as a 'philistine'. Through her nature, Fleda is unable either to prevent the marriage or arrange an accommodation between the disputants.

2nd Level Synopsis (by Chapter)

1

Mrs Gereth is enduring a weekend at Waterbath, the ugly, overstuffed country house of the Brigstocks, because she suspects that her only son Owen wishes to marry the vulgar Mona Brigstock. She finds a kindred spirit in a young unattached woman of somewhat straitened circumstances, Fleda Vetch.

2

Back in London, Mrs Gereth takes Fleda under her wing to give her experience of Poynton, the Jacobean house filled with art treasures collected by Mrs Gereth and her late husband, ownership of which has now passed by will to Owen.

Henry James himself famously wrote scenarios about everything. The woman he met at last night's concert. The couple bickering at a luncheon. The story he heard third hand. His mind was always in narrative mode. He tested and decorated story endlessly, constantly. His *Notebooks* are a wonder to read.

Some writers prefer to compose lists of "beats" (steps of action), rather than to summarize narratively. (I often do both, finding the beats to be a good way to dissect the summary.) Beats work especially well when your passage is full of robust action and you want to track what's going on. They are also helpful when you recognize that a passage is too slow and un-eventful (usually because of too much interiority and too little action). Writing the beats of a scene will reveal to you that it is a weak passage. Here is such an example from a writer's first draft:

1. Jean is at her computer, looking at photographs.
2. She thinks about her career as a photographer unhappily.
3. She hears a car coming up the driveway and thinks about how long it has been since she and Daniel were a couple.
4. She closes her computer and stands up and looks out the window.
5. She feels ugly and wishes she had worn something different.
6. She lets Daniel in the house. (And so on.)

Once this writer had gone through her scene, she recognized how little was going on, how slow the action was, and how much was interior but not very intriguing. Here is her revision of the beginning of the scene:

1. Jean, awaiting her lover, stands at her study window observing two birds who appear to be fighting over a nest.
2. Suddenly aware of her dowdy at-home outfit, she starts unbuttoning her blouse and turns to go to her bedroom.
3. She hears Daniel's truck as he turns into her driveway.
4. She greets him at the door, blouse half undone.

As a scenario, this would read:

Jean is watching birds at her window while awaiting the arrival of her old lover, Daniel. She realizes how dowdily she is dressed and begins unbuttoning her blouse, intending to change. At that moment, Daniel turns into her driveway, and she meets him at the door, blouse undone.

As you probably discern, this would be a short scene, not a lot longer than the scenario, but with details and a sense of movement.

Scenarios are helpful before writing, as a *planning* tool; they are also helpful after writing, as an *analytical* tool. If you are writing a scenario before writing text, keep a tight focus on action. If you can pin down what is going to happen in the scene, sequence, or chapter, it frees some of your consciousness from that part of the invention. The writing itself can be raw, sketchy, clumsy, and still serve your purpose of putting ideas down so they don't fly away.

If you are summarizing what you have already written, think of your story as being somewhere in the draft, and write a summary of the story you meant to tell or want to tell. If this produces an alternative version, consider whether it is better than the original. *In revision, the scenario serves as a transition from the old version to the new.* Think of the scenario as a map of what you will write in the new draft. In fact, you can also "write" a scenario visually, by laying out a scheme that represents steps in the story, or a circle with spokes, a house plan with rooms, and so on. The idea is to create a cheat sheet that reminds you of the key elements of whatever narrative component you are summarizing.

Compressing your story is efficient. It is also an excellent heuristic, enabling you, through trial and error, to grasp something that you couldn't quite define before. The harder it is for you to do, the more you need to do it!

See "Notes on my revision scheme for *A Chance to See Egypt*" under Sample Scenarios in the Resources section.

EXERCISE

❑ Write a summary of a scene from your draft. You can also practice by summarizing scenes or chapters from a published novel. The skill will be important as you progress in planning your revision. I usually have my students who are writing novels write a chapter-by-chapter summary of an entire published novel, and they tell me it is eye-opening and empowering.

Try reducing the summary to a single sentence, a "caption." In the above example, it would be, "Jean greets her lover, blouse undone."

Reading your draft

Before you begin revision, read your manuscript. Yes, again.

Take the manuscript someplace you don't usually work: a coffee shop, a library, a park bench. Tell yourself this isn't the time to criticize or fret; you aren't going to make notes. Just read. If you can read it in a sitting, all the better; don't let it go more than another day or two.

Here is the big question about your novel draft: Is it what you thought it would be?

Even though the story is sooo familiar to you, there should be a kind of surprise at the end: Did I write that? There should be a satisfaction and release, followed by a buoyancy and urgency to get back to work; but there might be a sick feeling that you've missed the boat.

If the story is weak, you can't fix it by fussing with sentences. Don't confuse the need to rewrite sentences with the quality of the story itself. Step away. Come back to it the next day. If you still feel disappointed *in the story itself*, you may have to rethink the story. You have to believe in it. Follow it. Find it. *This is what revision is about.*

If it is the writing that disappoints you, tell yourself fixing comes later. Don't let your self-consciousness get in the way of your courage. If the story is there, you can strengthen the way it is told in the next draft. I don't know how to tell you the difference between enough and not enough, but my measure lies in passion.

I think you'll know if you shouldn't carry on, but it won't be because the first draft isn't great writing. (Sometimes a failed draft is written well. Sad, huh?) A good story can look like a holy mess in the first draft. It can be hidden behind ellipses and muddle. If you still like it, if you want to tell it, keep going. Start over. The questions and exercises in this book will provoke new ideas.

Write fifty scenarios if you need to. Draw cartoons. (Seriously.) Write another draft. I can think of a lot of writers who took five, six, or more years to get their books written—and published.

As long as you feel that somewhere in there you have put down the bones of a good story, you are ready to move forward. If you feel uneasy, or just plain downhearted, but you don't feel defeated, give yourself a break and start writing scenarios. Or take the heart of a chapter and write a short short story. The impulse is there. If you have a patient friend, try telling the story, letting the person ask questions. But get a pretty solid story in your head before you try to revise how you tell it. That doesn't mean that you have to recite all the details. You need a strong sense of the protagonist's central dilemma and the big events. Then you can work it out, using the information and exercises in this book.

Asking for feedback

If you want to ask someone to read the story, please, please tell the person to read it without a pencil in hand. You don't need little notes and circled spelling errors. Remind the reader that you just got your ideas down, that you know it can be better with more work. All you need is a general reaction. I'd say to this person, *Here's all I'm asking you to do. Tell me:*

1. Were you ever confused? Bored? (*Yes, I need to know.*)
2. Were there moments when you felt immersed in the story?
3. What would you tell another person if asked what the novel is about?
4. What would you say was the best scene or passage?

All of your attention for now is on your *story*.

How much work is this going to be?

How much work it'll take is entirely up to you. Follow my advice in this book section by section, considering each concept as I discuss it, considering your manuscript. The order I've used starts with *describing* what you have done, then moves to *evaluating* enough of it to make a decision about what you need to do next. Choose the tasks that seem most relevant to you. I think of myself as a coach and I offer a lot of help, but everyone won't need the same things from my book.

The thing is, you've put in a lot of time developing your story into a workable draft, so this isn't the time to hurry. Be open to discovery, chagrin, exuberance, fatigue. Be willing to take the time to *think*.

Two important notes

1. *Be sure that you have at least one novel on hand* as you read this book, other than your own manuscript. Choose ones that you know well or read recently. I refer to F. Scott Fitzgerald's *The Great Gatsby*, so you may want to read it as part of your study. One of the most interesting things to study in that book is how Gatsby's biography is revealed. Fitzgerald wrestled with this a lot, and, taking the advice of his great editor, Maxwell Perkins, he broke up the information and delayed its revelation instead of dumping it all in the beginning.

You may prefer a book that is more contemporary, more like what you have in mind for your own novel. When I talk about a concept and present examples, look to the book you have chosen and identify the same concept as it relates to that story. If you feel that you are well-read and can call up examples on your own, you may not need to work with a single text. It just depends on how studious you are. The most important text, of course, is your own. *Keep model novels at hand as you read and work.*

2. *Write your responses* to questions and exercises; write your concerns about your text and new ideas about possible revision ideas. Don't count on remembering. You have several ways to record revision ideas:

    a. You can keep notes on index cards. Key them to the section that they relate to, such as:

        Aboutness: vision

        Timeline: backstory

        Novel world

    b. You can write on Post-it Notes and stick them on the relevant passages in this book and in your bound manuscript.

    c. Write on the back of your bound manuscript pages, across from the relevant pages of text. Underline, block out chunks of text, etc. It's really important to record your thoughts as you go along. Later you can go through everything and see what makes sense and how your observations help you make decisions about your manuscript.

d. You can use the loose manuscript pages, which you have organized in sets of chapters, when you begin cutting things up and moving them around for revision purposes. I do advise you to compile your notes on the bound copy, however, as the point of having loose pages is to be free to jumble them about.

The important thing is: Don't expect to remember your reactions to these exercises. *Write them down.*

The long perspective

I've assumed that my reader is writing a novel or wants to. But maybe you want something else: to be a novelist. Maybe you are starting on a life's journey. If so, I think this book will help, because if you study all of it, if you read all the novels and craft books I recommend, if you make all these concepts and skills your own, you will have a strong foundation. Many of the ideas I am exploring are never discussed comprehensively (if at all) in classes or workshops. There isn't enough time, and there is an overemphasis on short fiction, for practical reasons. Some concepts are mentioned, of course, across disparate texts, such as books about plotting, and you may end up comparing what different writers advise. Choose what makes sense to you and leave the rest aside for now. Writing doesn't follow a recipe. We aren't baking cakes here. Of course you may sometimes disagree with me; articulating why you see an issue another way is useful, too. *My main role is to give you a scheme for organizing your revision.* If you have read other books on writing novels, some topics will be familiar, though my vocabulary may be different. Some ideas will probably be new to you. Mostly, you will start to build your own strategies for writing and revising fiction.

Simply follow the general outline:

Describe your story concept and intention.
Describe the way you have put the story down.
Think about various structural issues.
Identify your areas of concern.
Articulate the goals of your revision.
Decide what goes, what stays, what gets written.
Make a plan.
Write.
Give your manuscript a loving gloss.

That's it!

EXERCISES

- ❑ Write a statement of intention. What do you hope to accomplish? How much time can you give to the effort? Do you have any kind of peer support? (Someone you can report your progress to? Another writer who is also using this book to revise her own manuscript?)
- ❑ Have you chosen at least one book you like, to work with as you go through the revision sections? Start by writing a short summary of the book—just a few sentences. Write down why you like the book, and be specific: characters? scenes? descriptions? structure of chapters? feeling of suspense?

One: A Close Look

Everything to follow is concerned with these three questions: *Who* is the story about? *What* happens? *Why* does it matter?

Description

What is the story?

1. Write a summary of the first draft.
2. State the subject of your novel in a single sentence.
3. State what your novel is about (action and effect).
4. State the vision or intention of your novel.
5. Describe the world of the novel.
6. Create timelines for foreground and backstory chronology.
7. Identify the most important backstory events.
8. Describe your protagonist in terms of agency, struggle, and transformation.

9. Describe your protagonist's fate and its relationship to your vision.
10. Describe your other major characters.

1. Write a summary of the first draft.

A few pages will suffice. You want to cover the main thrust of the plot and the nature of the protagonist and his or her driving force. Indicate how things are complicated and resolved. This is a working document for you, so try to be precise but don't worry about polish. Don't get caught up in "this happened, and then this happened . . ." Think of yourself as looking at the story from a more distant location.

See the broad movements of action, the larger complications. Mention the moments that matter most.

If writing the summary is difficult for you, set it aside and try again later in the day, or the next day. Don't try to "fix" the flawed summary draft; start over. You could go on to the next few exercises and come back to the summary. But do work until you get one that "feels right," one that captures what you have done, with a touch of what you mean to do.

Is this an unfamiliar or intimidating assignment?

It can be helpful to read reviews of novels, summaries on publishers' and booksellers' websites, jacket copy, etc. (A library will give you access to many options. Ask a research librarian for help finding reviews.) Each "take" on a novel has a slightly different purpose and strategy, but reading various summaries highlights for you the idea that each novel has an essence, a heart, a core; and you will see that a summary has a general pattern. I recommend going to a library and reading back issues of *Publishers Weekly*, which encapsulates forthcoming books on a weekly basis. The summaries aren't richly evocative the way good reviews are in journals, and perhaps for that very reason they are instructive. The reviews aren't style models, but they can give you a huge array of samples of summaries. There are several journals that review for librarians, including *Kirkus Reviews*. You can also get a good idea of how to summarize by reading the plot overviews in study guides to various novels.

If you feel drawn to make some changes in the story, the summary is a good place to test them. Don't feel chained to your draft; you have begun the steps that take you to a revision. Or you might write a summary of what you have, *print it out*, and then annotate it with questions and comments in the margins.

Ask yourself:

1. Does my story sound "large enough" for a novel? Does it need at least sixty thousand words to be developed? (About two hundred manuscript pages, minimum.)
2. Does the summary sound dramatic?
3. Does it have a fascinating protagonist—someone a reader will want to follow through the book?
4. Is a question raised that takes a novel to answer?
5. Can I read the summary and put my finger on sentences that stand out as events—the things that should happen in scenes (fill up pages!) in the novel?

All those qualities probably won't have been developed in the first draft, but the potential has to be there. *A big part of revision is deepening the story. You can start by deepening the summary.*

If you are a little shaky about answering, *Yes, I've got what it takes*, you probably need to think about subplots (sequences involving secondary characters' actions and issues that crisscross and affect the main plot) and about a protagonist with bigger problems. (Both issues are discussed in this book.) You should go back to consider what made you think you wanted to write this story. Wrestle with it; make it reveal itself to you. Go ahead and work through the activities; the exercises will inspire new ideas and your story will plump up. (Write new summaries whenever you think you have a significant change of mind.) Think of yourself as building a dossier, a kind of case study of the story you are looking for. Keep writing new summaries.

To give you an idea, here are a few summaries from publishers' and booksellers' websites. Your summaries don't have to be elegant and could certainly be more forthcoming—you don't need to tease a reader with yours.

The Vegetarian by Han Kang

Before the nightmares began, Yeong-hye and her husband lived an ordinary, controlled life. But the dreams—invasive images of blood and brutality—torture her, driving Yeong-hye to purge her mind and renounce eating meat altogether. It's a small act of independence, but it interrupts her marriage and sets into motion an increasingly grotesque chain of events at home. As her husband, her brother-in-law and sister each fight to reassert their control, Yeong-hye obsessively defends the choice that's become sacred to her. Soon their attempts turn desperate, subjecting first her mind, and then her body, to ever more intrusive and perverse violations, sending Yeong-hye spiraling into a dangerous, bizarre estrangement, not only from those closest to her, but also from herself.

Celebrated by critics around the world, *The Vegetarian* is a darkly allegorical, Kafka-esque tale of power, obsession, and one woman's struggle to break free from the violence both without and within her. (Source: www.penguinrandomhouse.com.)

The Last Kashmiri Rose by Barbara Cleverly

In a land of saffron sunsets and blazing summer heat, an Englishwoman has been found dead, her wrists slit, her body floating in a bathtub of blood and water. But is it suicide or murder? The case falls to Scotland Yard inspector Joe Sandilands, who survived the horror of the Western Front and has endured six sultry months in English-ruled Calcutta. Sandilands is ordered to investigate, and soon discovers that there have been other mysterious deaths, hearkening sinister ties to the present case.

Now, as the sovereignty of Britain is in decline and an insurgent India is on the rise, Sandilands must navigate the treacherous corridors of political decorum to bring a cunning killer to justice, knowing the next victim is already marked to die. (Source: https://sohopress.com.)

The Last Painting of Sara De Vos by Dominic Smith

Smith's latest novel is a rich and detailed story that connects a seventeenth-century Dutch painting to its twentieth-century American owner and the lonely but fervent art student who makes the life-changing decision to forge it. . . .

This is a beautiful, patient, and timeless book, one that builds upon centuries and shows how the smallest choices—like the chosen mix for yellow paint—can be the definitive markings of an entire life. (Source: *Kirkus Reviews*.)

The Piano Maker by Kurt Palka

Helene Giroux arrives alone in St. Homais on a winter day. She wears good city clothes and drives an elegant car, and everything she owns is in a small trunk in the back seat. In the local church she finds a fine old piano, a Molnar, and she knows just how fine it is, for her family had manufactured these pianos before the Great War. Then her mother's death and war force her to abandon her former life.

The story moves back and forth in time as Helene, settling into a simple life, playing the piano for church choir, recalls the extraordinary events that brought her to this place. They include the early loss of her soldier husband and the reappearance of an old suitor who rescues her and her daughter, when she is most desperate; the journeys that very few women of her time could even imagine, into the forests of Indochina in search of ancient treasures and finally, and fatefully, to the Canadian north. When the town policeman confronts her, past and present suddenly converge and she must face an episode that she had thought had been left behind forever. (Source: penguinrandomhouse.ca.)

EXERCISES

❑ Read your summary. If it doesn't sound right to you, write it again.

❑ Start a file of summaries. Go to publishers' websites, booksellers' websites, and prepublication review journals like *Publishers Weekly* and *Library Journal*.

2. State the subject of your novel in a single sentence.

You will be asked many times to say what your novel is "about." There are several ways you might answer, and this is probably not the one you will choose, since people expect to hear about events. But it is helpful to articulate "aboutness" at the subject level as a starting point. *Madame Bovary*'s subject is the stifling narrowness of French middle-class life for a woman. *All Quiet on the Western Front*'s subject is the grim experience of ordinary German soldiers in World War I. The subject of *The Grapes of Wrath* is the migration of poor farm families during the Depression. The subject of *The Curious Incident of the Dog in the Night-Time* is a boy's determined struggle to overcome his limitations and expand his independence. The subject of Maggie Shipstead's *Seating Arrangements* is the culture of a WASP family on an idyllic Cape Cod island. The subject of *More Than Allies* is mothers trying to raise fatherless sons; *When the Emperor Was Divine* is about a family in a World War II internment camp for Japanese residents on the West Coast. *All the Pretty Horses* is about rootless teenage boys looking for an ideal West in Mexico. *The Scarlet Letter* is about a woman's experience as an adulteress in the cruelly repressive Puritan environment. *The Piano Maker* is about a French widow's journey from great loss to redemption in Canada.

None of these statements tell you what happens, but each establishes a subject for a novel to explore, suggests characters and setting, and easily nudges you further toward a statement of "what happens." I daresay a subject statement already says enough about your story to test the interest of potential readers. Try it out on anyone who will listen.

I could pare the statements down further, same order, and say these books are about: ennui; war; poverty; autism and adolescence; class systems; broken families; prejudice; coming-of-age; persecution; fate and cruel environment; but we are also thinking of context (discussed shortly).

Try to state the subjects of novels that you know. Lots of them. Why? Because it is possible to write a long novel and think it is about a lot of things—marriage and death, love and betrayal—when truly there is no basic subject. You want to train yourself to grasp the story idea. A love story, for example, takes place in a context. So is the subject the rivalry of families? The dissolution of community in the suburbs? The return to civilian life of soldiers home from war? It isn't enough to say a book is a love story, a crime story, a family story. Something is special about the time, the place, the characters; find a way to touch on that in the statement of your subject. Think of yourself as putting a lens in focus.

Is this just an exercise? Maybe. But my students who have the hardest time with it are the ones with the fuzziest notion of their stories. And if reviewers and readers talk about your novel when it is published, you can be sure they will be saying, "It's about—" Do you think they will know what to say if you didn't know? (Take a look at the way novels are described in the abbreviated descriptions in magazines like *Vogue*, *Vanity Fair*, *Oprah*, *The New Yorker*, etc.)

SUBJECT YIELDS IDEA

Flaubert wrote a novel after reading about a small-town French physician's wife who killed herself. In *Walking Dunes* (teenagers in West Texas in 1959) I wrote about a boy from a working-class family who faces ethical choices he isn't prepared to deal with. The idea for the novel arose from reflections on my own adolescence, and especially from my memories of a boy who was my friend, a person of great promise who killed himself in his early thirties. In *All the Light We Cannot See*, Anthony Doerr wrote about a blind French girl and a young Hitler Youth whose lives cross in World War II. In *The Indian Bride*, mystery writer Karin Fossum wrote about murder in a Norwegian village (what happens when an immigrant bride is murdered immediately upon arrival to join her husband). In the popular Maisie Dobbs novels (e.g., *Leaving Everything Most Loved*) by Jacqueline Winspear, the protagonist, trained in World War I as a spy, is always caught up in political and social undercurrents: London between world wars, England and Germany during World War I and after; India, Egypt. I heard Swedish author Henning Mankell speak at Chicago's Printers Row Book Fair about his series of mysteries. He said they were about the incursion of evil into the beauty and solitude and peacefulness of Sweden.

This was in 2004, and his talk came to seem prescient as, in subsequent years, Scandinavia became deeply embroiled in economic and cultural challenges.

These considerations of subject really are about developing a rich base for a story to be told in. *Think of this stage as finding rich loam for planting your story.* Rich or poor? Big city or small village? War or peace? High finance or western ranching? Immigrants moving into Missoula? Aliens into St. Louis? Missionaries in the Congo? Trying to define something interesting and specific and full of possible conflict helps you to develop your story in a place and time where what other people believe and want affects your characters; where other things are going on in the community; these are the attributes that make your story robust. What "matters" in a novel needs to matter both specifically and broadly. The reader has to feel with the protagonist, but also with the world of the novel. It's obvious why there are so many novels set in wartime, so many adventure stories. We'll talk about this more when we talk about context.

Think of yourself as a pilgrim on a long trek: You really do need a passion before you walk very far. Ask yourself:

Why do I want to write this novel? What is it about the subject that inspires or drives me to this story? (Does it tie into something in my family experience? Something that I aspire to? Something that scares me?)

Why am I a good writer to tell this story? (Special knowledge? Special interest? Love of "digging" into history? Experience with some aspect of the story?)

What do I know—or what am I willing to learn—that will make a good story?

Exercises

- ☐ State the subject of a novel you know. Think about how the novel develops it. Do this with several novels. (Don't expect it to be an easy task.)

❑ List some of the things you had to research in order to write your story. When did you realize there was deep story in the subject? Do you need to do further research for your revision? If so, try to narrow the focus by writing out questions and seeking the answers.

❑ Read some descriptions of novels on booksellers' websites. State the subject of each.

❑ Make a list of writers you have liked enough to read at least two of his or her books. State the subject of each book. Is this a writer with a theme you see across various novels, or does the author totally change the realm of subject matter? (There's no right or wrong answer. Writers do tend to do one or the other sort of thing in selecting subjects for their novels.)

❑ Name some writers you think of as "writers of" some subject or theme. For example, Jodi Picoult writes about social issues that challenge families. Robert Goddard favors mysteries set in the late nineteenth and early twentieth century. Ann Patchett writes about wildly different subjects, reinventing herself as an author over and over. Kent Haruf wrote about common folk living in small towns. Margaret Atwood, with over forty works of fiction, has covered a lot of ground, but several of her books have visionary, otherworldly, sometimes terrifying subjects. Alice Munro imbues her Canadian "ordinary people" characters with deep inner lives that reflect history, culture, and psychology—as well as the fallibility of memory.

❑ Imagine yourself as a "writer of books about—." What subjects intrigue you? What would you want readers to say about your books? How would you be identified? By subject? By writing style? What makes you different?

3. State what your novel is about (action and effect).

The goal here is to be able to speak about your novel succinctly in a way that indicates not what the subject of the novel is, but what actually happens. Your statements become stars to guide you. You think, *What next?* and your statement suggests direction. You review a scene and ask, *Did I illuminate my aboutness?* Your ideas become concrete. My students tell me that once they go through this process, laying out sequences of scenes under each of the two parts, and then reducing the whole exercise to a single statement of aboutness, they go around with it thrumming in their brain! It really does become the North Star. But it can take a lot of false starts to find the right way to describe a novel's "aboutness."

This approach considers two aspects of the novel, then puts them together. One is about event, the other is about character emotions and behaviors.

The first statement is focused on *action*. (What events occur that have consequences?)

The other statement is focused on *affect* (What are the emotions and psychological states in the protagonist that are altered by events? How is behavior shaped?) and *effect* (What does this lead the protagonist to do?).

In the following examples I have included notes about what happens in a sample of novels to develop the statements. *Strong statements of aboutness always suggest event.* Note that the point of developing these two statements is to parse the story in a way that helps you identify the threads of plot and subplots. This is a template, not an elevator pitch. That said, when I work with students on developing queries, we start here.

EXAMPLE 1 *(Plain Seeing)*

The story is about:

a. what happens when a girl loses her mother in adolescence (*she grows up with unanswered questions; she makes immature life choices; she goes in search of her mother's story*)

and

b. what happens when a woman is locked in grief about the past and can't love her family in the present (*she seeks fulfillment in affairs; she withholds true commitment to her husband; she fails as a mother when her daughter most needs her; she searches for meaning*)

Then you can collapse the two parts (the events and the emotions) into a single aboutness statement that describes the novel: A woman whose obsession with her dead mother's mystery has ruined her marriage and her relationship with her teenage daughter goes on a search for her mother's true story.

EXAMPLE 2 *(Opal on Dry Ground)*

The story is about:

a. what happens when a woman's divorced daughters move in with her (*she tries to direct their lives, right down to making their beds*) and

b. what happens when the mother feels responsible for her daughters' lives (*she neglects her new husband; she incessantly mourns her own mother's death; she mixes her own emotions with her daughters'*)

Aboutness statement: A woman's divorced daughters resist her efforts to remake their lives, finding their own roads to independence and leaving her to construct her own life without them.

EXAMPLE 3 *(The Scarlet Letter)*

The story is about:

a. what happens when a young Puritan woman has a child by an unidentified man not her husband (*she is reviled and shunned, but she makes a life for herself and her daughter, while her absent husband secretly seeks retribution*) and

b. what happens when the persecuted woman is a stoic free-thinker (*she overcomes shame through her strength of character, her compassion, and her good works*)

Aboutness statement: Despite persecution and isolation for her illegitimate pregnancy, a Puritan woman of strong character makes a Christian life for herself and her child.

EXAMPLE 4 (from a student manuscript)

The story is about:

a. what happens to a family when druggie parents lose their sanity and their children grow up without guidance (*there are incidents with police and jail; a couple bouts of homelessness; only one daughter graduates from high school; the mother dies of an overdose*) and

b. what happens when a woman thinks she should have been able to "fix" the broken family, even though she was herself a wounded child (*she fails in relationships; she gets overinvolved in a brother's shaky life; she has to decide whether to carry a child to birth*)

Aboutness statement: A woman in early pregnancy is unexpectedly reunited with her troubled brother, whose low spirits and bad acts threaten to dismantle the fragile life she has constructed after their unspeakable childhood.

BRIEFLY, HERE ARE a few more from recent students; they are works in progress, but each has the nugget of a viable premise for a story.

A historical novel: When a widow takes in boarders in order to keep her house, she is drawn into the lives of poor, exploited women, and she joins them in their struggle for workers' rights, searching for her place in a world where you can be beaten for seeking a living wage.

A historical fantasy: An orphaned boy is raised by a powerful monk to be the warrior-protector of a future empress and must reconcile his role with his love of and fear for her.

A young adult novel: A thirteen-year-old girl, the sole survivor of a car crash that killed her entire family, is sent to live with an uncle she doesn't know.

A historical novel, World War II era: A young man who sat out the war in America with relatives returns to rural Germany and what is left of the family farm, and finds that a girl he loves is accused of having betrayed the community to the Nazis.

In each statement, you can see the potential movement of action, and events in the story that develop the statements of aboutness. Another way to think of the two parts of the story statement is that they are *event* and *pulse*. Event means *things happen*, arising from circumstances, situation, and character choices. The character's behavior occurs in a kind of river of feeling, a pulse that drums beneath the story. You engage the reader with events; you captivate the reader with character.

THIS IS AS good a time as any to bring up the notion of a novel being either *plot driven* or *character driven*. We'll spend more time on this later, but keep the issue in mind. *A novel always has to have a pleasing balance of plot (action) and character. Things have to happen; what happens has to have meaning for characters.* In a plot-driven novel, what is happening in linked sequences is the key focus. In a character-driven novel, who the protagonist is becoming is the primary focus—how the person is responding to events in a way that changes something about who she is. (In any really good novel, you have a compelling protagonist *and* a captivating plot.) So I am differentiating between story and plot, although to do so is somewhat artificial.

Story is what the narrative is about: what it says about life and how it illustrates it in event.

We use the word in that way all the time. ("What a story that old man's life was." "You won't believe the story I heard this weekend." "The stories I read about the stranded refugees make me weep." "I've heard that story before." And so on.) It can be organized in any way—it does not have to be chronological. *Plot is the constructed sequence of causally related events.* The critic Peter Brooks says, "Plot . . . is the design and intention of narrative, what shapes a story and gives it a certain direction or intent of meaning." *Plot is the arrangement of the story so that it makes sense and has an effect.* Though plot, too, can hold and reveal elements of story history in ingenious ways, it has as its spine a chronological arrangement of incident (first this, then that), because that is the Western way of conceiving story. *Plot is all about forward motion.* This is true even when the structure of the novel is built around the revelation of past events. The story-driven novel (character is paramount) may have a tight plot underlying its development, but the plot is revealed in a rich context of character and story world. I do hasten to say that a plot-driven novel can be a terrific—and literary—read if it has strong characters. Consider the Wallander mysteries by Henning Mankell. I would certainly identify them as plot driven, each focused on solving a crime and illustrating police procedure. At the same time, the weary, philosophical, touchy, solitary Inspector Wallander is drawn with psychological acuity, and over the course of the series, growing older, Wallander not only becomes increasingly weighed down by work and life and relationships, he also begins to lose his cognitive faculties. His personality and behavior, however, are not the structural engine of the novels; crime is. Similarly, Michael Connelly's Detective Harry Bosch novels have an overall arc in his search for his mother's killer, his inability to compromise with corruption and ineptitude, and his absolute sense of justice—that every victim deserves it, regardless of class or occupation. But the novels are about solving crimes.

So consider: Is the narrative driven by forces outside the protagonist? Major events, disasters, venomous villains, pressure from others' demands, and so on? All novels have a chain of events that are linked causally. Something happens so that something else happens. When the emphasis is on plot, the spectacle of events unfolding is more important than the character with the problem that arises out of them. In thrillers, for example, the hero is usually someone called upon to solve a crisis; it isn't necessary for him to change, only for him to step up. A way of describing such a plot might look like this: situation + circumstances → produce plot → produces pressure on character. Certainly it is possible to write a novel with plenty of action, adventure, and conflict, and still have a story solidly based in character. But what does that mean?

Primarily it means that character isn't a pawn of the plot. Character-centered stories respect the mystery of personhood, and the influence of life experience and basic traits on how a person behaves and faces challenge. The simplest way to put it is that in this kind of story, character + circumstances → produce situation → produces plot. The question isn't always what is going to happen next, so much as: Why is this person doing this? How will she choose the right thing? Given who she is, what can she do? What will she have to overcome in order to solve her problems or reach her goals? Who will she be, in the end? How do her choices affect those around her? Novels are wonderful vehicles for character exploration, and, for that matter, the exploration of ideas, not by aimless musing, but by plots that arise and are constructed because of who the protagonist is. A novel is a presentation of lives lived on the page.

If you go back to my examples, you'll see that the stories are character centered. Of course there's no reason that a character can't be the heart of a story that also has a rousing good plot!

The universally accepted great example is *The Great Gatsby*, wherein an intricate and inevitable plot carries the revelation and destruction of a character who, from the beginning, has nowhere to go but the hell his desires send him to. (By the way, the book is also a wonderful example of revision; Fitzgerald worked hard and made many changes, always with a vision in mind of how he would write a book for the ages. Look for an edition of the novel that includes a good introduction.)

Chances are you have a natural inclination toward one or the other approach—plot or character—to conceiving a novel. By recognizing what it is, you can make your scheme strong, and also be sure plot and character are balanced pleasingly. Furthermore, you may learn that your natural instinct is different from what you thought you were doing. If you write great scenes and enjoy moving things along, your work probably has commercial promise; that doesn't mean it can't be elegantly written. It doesn't mean it can't have a fascinating protagonist. It just means you aren't as limited by literary intentions as you maybe thought you were.

EXERCISES

- ❑ Write statements of *action* and *effect* for novels that you know. For each novel, consider: Is it primarily a novel of story or of plot?
- ❑ Write statements of *action* and *effect* for your novel. List some of the events that develop each part of the statement. Then collapse your work into a single sentence that sums up the story. (This is isn't easy. It will take a lot of time and tries.)
- ❑ Write your statement of the aboutness of your novel in large script and post it above your workspace. Look at it often. Tweak it.

Is your novel governed by story or plot?

4. State the vision or intention of your novel.

Think of what happens in your story as being governed in two ways: by the "agency" (power, intention) of the character; and by the "world" of the story. This task asks you to consider what you believe about agency. A characteristic problem in apprentice novels is that the protagonist is acted upon more than he acts. Even in the most controlled circumstances, your character must make choices (and mistakes). Whether the character directs his own fate to happy consequence is a decision in your hands—and it arises from your vision of the world of the novel. Emma Bovary certainly made her own bed and laid the path to her death in a social context where she could never have had what she wanted. Her dreams didn't fit her circumstances, but she couldn't accept the reality. That was how Flaubert saw her. What makes the story powerful instead of melodramatic is the precision and intricacy of the narrative, and, of course, the revolutionary way he conveyed Emma's voice.

The vision can be stated in a *dramatic premise* that is proven by the action of the story. This use of the word "premise" comes from the esteemed playwright and critic Bernard Grebanier. It isn't an absolute; it isn't a tenet. It is an understanding of human nature that is proven *in this particular story* as developed by conflict and its outcome. It is the result of the protagonist's journey.

The premise should be stated in terms of the protagonist's actions and fate. Think of it as what the protagonist learns.

Examples

Fixating on past grievances impedes a full and present life.
Living one's life as a pretender becomes intolerable and the revelation of the truth frees one to live more happily.
Running to the safety of home from the difficulty of one's adult life only complicates things, and one must grow up and face reality to solve problems.

Seizing power ruthlessly leads to estrangement and loss.

Compassion (caring for others) leads to forgiveness.

Risky adventure leads to painful maturing.

Even in the face of persecution, a person of strong character who struggles can prevail.

Habits of timidity and self-doubt paralyze progress; courage builds potential.

Eccentricity—a gift, not a fault—leads to unexpected success.

If we run from that which we fear, we will fall to its power.

Following one's powerful and rightful ambition fuels achievement.

In each case, you can see that the premise presents: (a) *an action (in comprehensive terms) that* (b) *leads to* (c) *a state of being or outcome*. In a single sentence you can see possible story development. I've had fun with workshop groups, giving them a premise, and having trios conceive of a plot, then comparing the various interpretations. In your own writing, you can do this, too, as a way of making yourself ask: *What if?* It is a way to come up with some fresh ideas, while questioning your own beliefs about people's responsibilities in a world that is full of consequences.

A novelist creates a world of the story, and that world has its own governing rules. This is most evident in genre novels such as fantasy, science fiction, romance, historical novels, Christian novels, and mysteries, but I believe that any novel needs a conceived and constructed environment for its story. (This has surprised many of my students, who hadn't thought of making up a setting.) Of course there is terrific variance, especially culturally. For example, Scandinavian crime novels almost always have a villain who is psychologically disturbed, as if the culture doesn't want to accept that evil can come from greed, envy, lust, and pride, but must instead always be the work of the insane. Mysteries set in major American cities inevitably involve corruption at high levels. Romance ends in marriage, but the route—and the defining of relationships—has changed enormously in the last twenty years. Absurdity—situations where arbitrary rules make no sense—abounds in places where people are oppressed.

At first it may be less obvious in the mainstream novel that there is a governing vision, but every story is a proof of what the writer believes about how life works—or should work, or could. In Jacqueline Winspear's Maisie Dobbs novels, integrity, intellect, comradeship, intuition, and courage always solve the mystery and end the danger. In the novels of Kent Haruf (e.g., *Plainsong*, *Benediction*), life challenges the mundane routines of decent people, and they pull from their deep compassion and righteous instincts the courage to shake up their own lives. (Haruf's last novel, *Our Souls at Night*, shocked me, because the characters—an elderly couple—couldn't overcome the family forces against them.) In my own *Walking Dunes*, a poor young man doesn't get what he wants, or perhaps better said, doesn't want what he gets. In the world of that novel, 1959 West Texas, you are born a have or have-not, and it takes tremendous courage and luck to choose the direction of your life if you lack resources. The story "proves" this in David's ambiguous situation at the end, but also in the different choices made by his gutsy friend Patsy, a girl who is determined to make an artistic life on her own terms. And the author's philosophy is evident, too, in that David's poor choices are governed by his dreams of wealth and success, while Patsy's are governed by her desire to be an authentic person.

In Julie Otsuka's *When the Emperor Was Divine*, Japanese immigrants and Japanese Americans are interned in camps during World War II. To survive, one had to be compliant; to endure, one had to maintain dignity without defying authority. One could say that the vision of the novel is cruel, but I think rather that "the world" isn't the camps, but the family, where integrity and familial and ethnic solidarity sustain the characters. One's goodness, in that world, isn't defined by strangers and rulers but by selfhood. It exists within.

In *The Scarlet Letter*, a sin (adultery) made public (by the pregnancy) in seventeenth-century Boston inevitably wreaks humiliation and ostracism for the sinning woman, but in Hawthorne's vision, great strength of character, revealed over years in good works, compassion, and a humble but strong sense of self, lead the sinner to a decent life. The truly punished are men—the vengeful, scheming old husband and the guilty but secretive young minister who fathered the woman's child. Hawthorne's subject was the intolerance of Puritan reformers, but Hawthorne's vision of their repressive practices in contrast to Hester Prynne's intelligence and strong character allowed him to illuminate the role of psychology in the way one is affected by fate.

In *The Great Gatsby*, ambition and success and lavish generosity aren't enough for Gatsby to win back the love of Daisy, who is married to a wealthy and cruel man. Fitzgerald was much driven by his love for his own wife, Zelda, who was a mismatch, and by his ambition, which was often in tension with his sense that society had gone mad with greed. In the *Gatsby* world, good men don't win, rich men do, but because the story is told by the thoughtful young Nick, Fitzgerald could also suggest the hope for men of integrity, compassion, and common sense.

So one way to think of vision in the novel is to ask yourself:

How should people treat one another?

How should the earth's goods be shared?

What responsibilities do families (or strangers) have for one another?

What happens when such "goodnesses" are violated?

What do you think an individual is capable of under great stress?

One way or another, you are inevitably making a case for how life works, so you might as well be conscious of what you are doing. Are you exploring how things shouldn't be, or how they should be? Or perhaps how they would be if . . . ? When you think about these questions, you will surely find that you have beliefs about nature, governance, wealth, sex, religion, love, and more that affect the choices you make in your stories. For that matter, you have beliefs about the nature of fiction itself. I'm not saying a novel should be a sermon, nor that your belief in good things means goodness wins every battle, but I do believe that, whether on purpose or not, fiction (good or bad) is a representation of life, and it's worth thinking about what you believe, and what kind of experience of life you are showing the reader. (If a novelist argues that this isn't so in his case, I reply: Then your refusal to define your vision defines it for you, with no governing philosophy or psychology to create coherence.)

Louise Erdrich recently revised her novel *The Antelope Wife* because, looking back across a decade since it was published, she saw that she could deepen its theme and make it more what she meant for it to be; she felt maturity had sharpened her understanding of her story. She is truly a writer driven by vision.

Are you writing about how the world *is*? Or how it *could* be? Or how it *should* be? What effect on the reader are you striving for?

EXERCISES

❏ Think of a novel that you feel has a powerful vision. Find events in the book that reflect that vision. Is the underlying vision part of why you like the book?

❏ Consider writing a *credo* (a statement of belief). What would you like to help readers understand about human nature?

5. Describe the world of the novel.

IDENTIFYING CONTEXT AND SCOPE

Where does your novel take place? City? Suburbia? Academia? Distressed neighborhood? Utopia under siege? The back alleys of Ancient Rome? You very likely didn't so much choose the setting as have the setting choose you because of the story that came to mind. But setting is a powerful element of narrative. You want yours to be highly specific, logical, and in some way unique to your story. You want to think of what takes place inside and outside; in groups and not; in day or night. Consider the climate and landscape.

The world of the novel is the ground for the story. A story happens someplace. *It happens because circumstances come together to put events in motion. So start by conceiving of the right place for your story to happen.*

Start by thinking of writers whose work is remarkable for how it uses setting: the rough country and the rough society of *All the Pretty Horses*; the stifling mediocrity and leaden boredom of small-town life in *Madame Bovary*; the greed and amorality of *The Great Gatsby*'s Long Island society illustrated in the estates, and the filth of its "Valley of Ashes"; the suffocating heat, barren landscape, and threatening "otherness" of Paul Bowles's *The Sheltering Sky*. In *Fools Crow*, James Welch not only presents the world of the Lone Eaters in the Two Medicine Territory of Montana, he portrays the loss of that way of life. And in *Winter in the Blood*, he shows what modern life is like on the Fort Belknap Reservation in Montana. The emptiness of the landscape and the grittiness of the small towns evoke the tragedy of what was lost. Umberto Eco's *The Name of the Rose* certainly has plot (heresy and murder), but what made the novel fabulously successful was its setting—a medieval abbey—and the cunning brilliance of its protagonist, a monk. In each of these books, the story could take place only in such a setting; the setting could produce only such a story. This is the feeling of inexorability that a great novel creates, that you want to create.

Consider the world of your novel. What is going on where your characters live? How does personal story resonate with public story? How is an individual constrained or supported by society? What political, economic, social, or natural forces are crossing one another? What is the nature of social reward and punishment? *How do you show these things and how do they influence the events and the characters?* Start with family; every family has a construct of rules and rewards and punishments. What happens when a family member defies those rules? What happens when a person "overreaches"? What happens when love crosses "boundaries" of sex, ethnicity, class? If you take the time to answer these questions about your story, you may discover new possibilities for character and plot.

Context

Context has tremendous power in the novel; readers love to be immersed in places and circumstances that are exaggerated, pushed beyond ordinary limits. In *All the Pretty Horses*, it is 1948 but once the two Texas boys cross the border into Mexico, they are in a world out of time, as surely as Alice in Wonderland. The boys have no history to help them understand the pride and mores of an aristocratic Mexican family, the cruelty and contempt of the people for the boys, or the extent of suffering they must endure.

Long Island (fashionable East Egg and unfashionable new-rich West Egg) isn't just the setting in *The Great Gatsby:* It is Fitzgerald's vision of a swath of American life at the time he was writing *Gatsby*. Tremendous changes have taken place in the nation's life: women coming out from the kitchen; business and industry creating great new wealth; a swelling resistance to immigration (sound familiar?). Strivers are reaching for wealth and status, insulting and threatening the people of old wealth. Fitzgerald's genius is to encapsulate so much of the culture in a very particular place, with characters who can be seen to represent excesses of the time, but who are fully developed as themselves, people you will never forget once you have read this book. At its heart is bighearted Gatsby, the ultimate self-made man, and Nick (the narrator), the ultimate contemplator, searching for meaning.

Adam Johnson won a Pulitzer Prize for *The Orphan Master's Son*, an amazing novel set in the horrific world of North Korea. His settings are so various and convincing you shiver and recoil, though the story is also about love and sacrifice and dignity in a place where none is publicly recognized.

To stretch yourself, think of how you can intensify setting: an ice storm, a rash of crimes, a broken electrical grid, an outbreak of Legionnaires' disease, soaring land prices. Small pressures matter, too: a leaking faucet, a fender bender, too many gray days, a sick pet. In *House of Sand and Fog*, Andre Dubus III's astonishing novel of divergent fates colliding, everything starts rolling because a young woman with a hangover doesn't open her mail. An ordinary California house becomes a place of tragedy because getting it, or losing it, means so much.

As an exercise, consider what would happen if you set your story in an entirely different place or time. Consider something outlandish, like a frozen outpost or a foreign city. Then come closer to the home of the novel, but change the neighborhood, the season, the year. How would that change what happens? If it wouldn't matter much, you aren't using setting.

Study a novel you like and analyze how setting influences the story. *Seating Arrangements*, by Maggie Shipstead, a WASP novel if there ever was one, could take place only in its setting or one just like it. A family convenes on an island off New England for the marriage of a daughter. It's a small world, and the exclusivity of the country club golf course is a major factor in the protagonist's unhappiness and anxiety. (He doesn't come from "old money," and no matter how much he earns, he doesn't belong to the wealthy aristocracy.) The nooks and crannies of the old family house provide places for rendezvous and unhappy discovery. The rehearsal dinner is the perfect place for revelations and stumbles. A men's club has all the claustrophobia and mustiness of the milieu that doesn't accept the protagonist.

Another WASP novel is Nancy Clark's comedy *The Hills at Home*. The Hills are a family; the place is their ancestral home in New England, where one relative after another shows up over a month's time. And stays. And stays. The house is dilapidated and overcrowded and everything takes place in it.

In *The Great Gatsby*, of course, Fitzgerald used his knowledge of Great Neck to create the contrasting worlds of the old rich, the new rich, the poor, and New York City. But what I especially love about the novel is how he uses weather to create emotional tone, such as Gatsby and Daisy's reunion in pouring rain. The setting of the Midwest even figures in, because Nick remembers it as a healthy contrast to the life he is observing on Long Island.

If you just start thinking about novels you love, you'll recognize how specific and memorable the settings are in good stories.

The most obvious problem I see in apprentice novels is a failure of imagination: too many things take place in too few settings. I once had a workshop group itemize settings in their manuscripts, and among twelve people, there were fifty-five scenes in kitchens or bedrooms! I challenged the group to move every kitchen scene to a setting that in some way aggravated or emphasized or contrasted with the conflict between characters, all of them to take place outside the characters' homes. The results were exciting—and riotous. A breakup that had involved broken dishes in a couple's kitchen got moved to supper in a church basement. A confrontation over an accusation of theft took place in traffic gridlock instead of at a dinner party. A teenage girl revealed her pregnancy at a piano recital. And Grandma had her heart attack while trying on scarves at a school bazaar.

Many aspects of setting change over the course of time, too, and therefore can change over the course of your story. You should exploit this characteristic. What was clean can be dirty;

what was dry can be wet; what was beautiful can be marred; what was full can be empty.

For example, there have been novels about the encroachment of gentrification or industry on neighborhoods or agricultural land. If you can identify something that is "moving in" on your story background, it can (a) create plot opportunities and (b) stand for thematic elements about change. *The Grapes of Wrath* of course came from Steinbeck's experience with the dispossession of tenant farmers in the Dust Bowl, and their migration to California. Jane Smiley's books are always replete with history, landscape, and climate; each is a panorama of a place and time, from Greenland to American farmland to horse farms to late-nineteenth-century California.

Setting works on a microlevel, too. Something as simple as a garden of flowers or vegetables can create a motif for the story, accenting the passage of time, the inevitability of ripeness and decay, etc. A character fraught with problems might also be battling blackberry vines against his back fence.

Scope

Scope is about span, extent, duration. Within the setting, a story can be claustrophobic or spacious. Similarly, time can feel generous or constricted. What you don't want is to let decisions about scope be happenstance. Ask yourself: How much time is being covered? Can you justify the time frame or was the decision the result of "that's just how long it takes"? What is the effect of time on the story? What feeling for time are you striving for?

Remember that whether the story takes place over a weekend (think of Ian McEwan's *Saturday*) or over years (*War and Peace*), it always has to give the reader the feeling of time moving forward across events. Try to imagine telling your story in a shorter time frame, or a longer one, and consider what would change. (Especially consider the effect of compression.) What would now be impossible? Would that matter? You may find that compression will heighten drama; or that longer development may yield a deeper story. As always, in revision the choice is a considered one.

I should point out that some writers treat setting very differently from what I am suggesting. Haruki Murakami is an obvious example, with his spare but evocative stories. If you aspire to that kind of lean prose, you'll learn to make deft strokes, too, not because you don't care about setting, but because you have a poet's instinct for image and suggestion.

Describe the world of your story in a sentence.

Describe the scope of your novel.

Describe the "rules" of your story world.

Exercises

- ❏ Think of other things about setting that aren't place: the music that plays in the story's background; news of the world and the community; the change in light as a season changes.

- ❏ Think, too, of using specific terms instead of general ones: geraniums, not big flowers; loafers, not just shoes. Specific identification (not overdone) increases the believability, the authority, of the text, and can sometimes carry notes of character—a man who lives alone and has a French press versus a more ordinary coffeepot.

- ❏ Think of the senses. *The Last Painting of Sara de Vos* by Dominic Smith is filled with smells. One of the characters is a painting restorer, and her beautifully described apartment is redolent of rabbit glue and spirits. The novel is also remarkable for its descriptions of New York City auction houses, jazz clubs, and even squash ball courts in two different eras.

- ❏ Be deliberate in choosing the season(s) in which your story takes place, and take advantage of what each suggests, whether it is the gray damp melancholy of a winter rain, or the promise of budding trees in spring.

❑ Think of novels you have liked for their settings. List the sites in which major scenes take place. How does the story come out of those settings? Or how does the setting reinforce action and emotion? If you can, be specific about actions that occur because of where the characters are.

❑ Play with ideas for changing aspects of setting in your novel. Consider what else would have to change in the story. Start with a single chapter: List every setting. Think how you could make the story more interesting or more dramatic in different settings.

❑ Skim your text for the objects you mention. Is it possible to be more specific? To use a more exact word? To describe it more succinctly? To mention color? To use the object?

❑ Go through the manuscript and write a tally of times of day when scenes take place. Do you exploit the changes in light? The background movement of people going off to work versus children on bicycles after school?

6. Create timelines for foreground and backstory chronology.

Timelines will be invaluable to you in sorting events and staying on track in the present time of the novel. Make two separate timelines, for "now" and "then." Concern yourself with your *protagonist* and the major line of the plot. (Consult your statement of aboutness and see how it is demonstrated in the novel's events.)

Now, I realize that you've already written a draft. You already have a foreground and background. You already put the past in there like ferns behind the flowers. So what are you to do?

Given that you have done a draft and know your story better

than you did when you started it, try doing these timelines *without referring to the draft*. In other words, use your best judgment *from this point in time and in your thinking* to identify the most important elements of the novel. Don't be shy about making changes. Your job right now is to describe the story as you know it; you may already be revising. You can check your draft after you make your timelines. If you do this and you recognize that your "best story now" is somewhat different from what you wrote in the first draft, you'll know that, before you do any rewriting, you'll need to identify new scenes to write and old ones to amend or discard. Write yourself notes on those blank pages in your bound manuscript. *Do not trust that you will remember.*

If you do the timelines from *what you are thinking now*, you should *also* do a representation of the timelines in your present draft. If there is a difference between the two, you'll see possibilities for revision.

Then, if you want to do it now, go through the draft and find the places where you brought in backstory. Visually block out the backstory with boxes or squiggles. You don't have to deal with the misalignment you see now. Make notes or write questions to yourself on the manuscript's blank pages. Keep going. Don't spend too much time on this, since the scenes may change anyway, but it is a good practice to review how you have used the past.

And by the way, for a quick look at masterful handling of present, near past, middle past, and distant past, see Ethan Canin's short story "The Year of Getting to Know Us," in *Emperor of the Air*. A commitment-phobic man goes to see his dying father and has to deal with his present relationship and the memory of his childhood. A story is a quicker study than a model novel, and yet there is a lot to learn in this one. You could actually use it as a template for a novel design; it isn't sophisticated, but it is elegant. It lends itself wonderfully to storyboarding. So make a copy of it and get your pens out.

USING THE FOREGROUND TIMELINE

When you look at the progression of events on your foreground timeline from the place where you open the novel, look for problems of repetition, such as similarity of events. (You should be focusing on the thread of events concerning the protagonist, at this stage.) You could do a run-through of the scenes, noting settings, for example. If the same conflict comes up over and over, you want to think about why that is so, and how the nature of the battle is shifting, if it is, and whether the stakes are getting higher, the fire hotter.

See what sequences emerge (the connections between events). You will look at these considerations in detail later, when you write a tagline for each chapter, and again when you develop a list of core scenes.

And oh yes—if you are writing a novel with multiple plotlines, you need both kinds of timelines for each plot and each subplot. Every plotline has to have its own tension and plot points, yet there has to be a kind of echo among the lines, places where the events converge. (They might converge in the past.) Creating a visual representation of the plot threads is helpful when you are trying to hold the whole thing in your head at one time. You can draw lines linking events, aligning chronology, and so on. The best way to understand how this works is to deconstruct a novel you admire.

If you are wondering how many events should appear on your timeline, you have to consider the scope of your novel. I suggest you start by spacing out six to ten major events (in pencil or with sticky notes) that comprise a general outline of the manuscript. Do they capture the general thrust of the story? Is something important left out? Play with the line. Think about what it takes to get from Event 1 to 2, from 2 to 3, and so on.

Post your timeline where you see it every day. Make it large enough to make notes on. (Post-it Notes are great because it's easy to make changes.) Before and after a chapter, check it against your timeline. Is one or the other askew? What needs to be adjusted?

BACKSTORY

With the past timeline, I wouldn't try to be so picky or detailed. Get down the main events in the protagonist's past, the things that have come up in your draft so far. Look for events or time frames that resulted in lasting fear or shame or resentment; anything that pushes conflict onto the present stage. You will come back to them after you work with the "present" timeline. One or two scenes will become important and you will make them hover over present events. Some events will simply fall away as irrelevant. You may be able to combine what happens in one event with another, and if you can, you probably should. Generally, less is more. Don't crowd the story with events that took place before it began. Seldom do you need to fill in the interim scene sequences; rather, you will want to note outcomes, reverberations of the major events, those things that still matter ten or fifty years later.

Sometimes, of course, the "past" of the novel is recent. In *The Arrivals* by Meg Mitchell Moore, everyone is thinking about something that happened last week or even yesterday; there's lots of anxiety and resentment, and so everything gets worked over in character thoughts. Very little is in the past: one character's husband had a one-night stand; another character's boyfriend left her. Otherwise, life is going on on the page, dragging the accruing baggage with it. As you are writing your story, you may discover that an event on the foreground timeline becomes something that carries on in the plot. "Now" becomes "just happened" and leads to the coming events. That's called complication, and it's good plotting.

Think of your "known story" as a continuum that began with "past events" (before the "now" of the story). There are novels that do not need a concrete past, that are entirely composed of present action. Sometimes the past is simply a catalyst, pushing the story into being, such as the death of a Texas boy's rancher grandfather in *All the Pretty Horses*. The past is done with quickly. Most novels have characters with baggage from prior life experience, and the *known story* becomes part of the *present story*. In Maggie Shipstead's *Seating Arrangements*, the protagonist is heavily burdened by a secret in his past, something that keeps him from ever feeling truly a part of the world he lives in. There are others who know his past, too, increasing his anxiety, rightly so. (The woes of not quite fitting in with old money! I never thought I would care, but I grew to like the protagonist.) What I like about this novel is the way the past presses against the protagonist, shapes his decisions and behaviors, without needing to blow up in some obvious revelation. Rather, the insistent pressure of the character's shame and fear (he never did anything wrong except come from the "wrong" people) push him to some really bad choices. *Seating Arrangements* would be a good novel to study if your story has a similarly cloudy backstory that a character can't escape. There is actually very little event in the past, but there is a lot of resonance from it in the present.

Old news

What often happens in novel drafts is that writers get ideas about the past while they are writing the ongoing present, and they get bogged down trying to invent, integrate, and balance these elements—making all of it up at the same time. They end up suffocating action with backstory. They lose the thread and the tension of now. This isn't fatal to a first draft; you can easily go through it and identify the elements of backstory that matter, pull them out and organize them, and then decide where and when you will introduce them in the revised version for greater effect. But you have to be able and willing to identify "then" and "now" and consider excising the past. This seems to be hardest to do in the beginning, when there is some primary urge to shove in history as a scaffold for the opening action of the story.

Finding the right time to bring up old news is a big part of the talent and the skill it takes to write a novel. The past love affair of Daisy Buchanan and Jay Gatsby is the very heart of *The Great Gatsby*, but we don't really hear about it until we are deep into the novel (chapter 4), when Daisy's friend Jordan tells the narrator, Nick. Gatsby's passion to regain Daisy's love springs from their relationship long ago, but the novel is very much about what is happening *now*. I remind you that the placement of that backstory late instead of early was a revision decision for Fitzgerald, based on his editor Maxwell Perkins's suggestion. He did not write the novel quickly—or only once.

INTERIM SEQUENCES: An example

Think in terms of major incident or event, as in the following hypothetical story about the breakup of a marriage and the subsequent death of a couple's child: the first part of the novel establishes big changes in Ellen's life. (I am talking only about the opening movement of my hypothetical novel.) Let's define three major events that launch and complicate (but do not yet resolve) the story:

1. *Tom leaves Ellen.*
2. *Son Jimmy's leukemia is diagnosed.*
3. *Ellen moves in with Mother.*

Every scene does not appear on your timeline, but every *major event* should, and those will occur in scenes. You are putting down *what must happen* in the story. Other scenes and summaries will provide the sequences that link the major scenes.

So, between our first and third events from above (*Tom leaves Ellen* and *Ellen moves in with Mother*), you might have scenes that can be grouped into three sets or *scene sequences*:

Event 1: Tom leaves Ellen

Sequence 1: Between Event 1 and Event 2

- ❏ *Ellen is packing, crying, and throwing out Tom's left belongings in big garbage sacks.*
- ❏ *She goes through a mortifying search for a cheaper place to live (possibly compressed in summary with scene fragments).*
- ❏ *Tom moves in with another woman.*
- ❏ *Jimmy reacts badly to his father's absence.*

and

Sequence 2: Between Event 1 and Event 2

- ❏ *Jimmy has what seems like a bout of flu, with bruising, and doesn't shake it.*
- ❏ *A school nurse suspects child neglect, which leads to a social worker's visit to Ellen's apartment.*
- ❏ *Tom shows up to confront Ellen and try to take Jimmy.*

and

Sequence 3: Includes Event 2

- ❏ *A first visit at the pediatrician's, followed by meetings with specialists and tests (here is a good place for narrative summary!).*
- ❏ *Tom's hostile accusations; a moment of parental reciprocal sympathy when leukemia is diagnosed.*

and

Event 3

❑ *Ellen's mother appears at Ellen's house with a van and moves Ellen and Jimmy to her house.*

❑ *In the middle of the night, in the bathroom, Ellen breaks down and sobs.*

The next event, which is the first complication in the middle section of the story, is Ellen being served with divorce papers and Tom's demand for custody of their son.

As you look over the series of scene captions you can imagine sitting down to write them, one after another. The captions do not necessarily represent scenes of equal length; some of the action could be presented as narrative summary. But you can see where the bigger moments are, and you can see how to get from one to the next.

These phrases represent a set of scene sequences: One scene leads to the next logically and moves the plot in arcs of story line. The sequence is like a little story. Reducing sections of your own manuscript to a scheme like this is a very good litmus test of its logic and coherence. You'll discover quickly if something is missing. It also can serve as an outline for rewriting.

So, after you have made the "broad strokes" timeline, and after you have done further evaluation of your draft, you can take each "set" on the timeline (two events) and establish the beats of scenes that come between, moving the plot from one situation to the next one. This is how you develop scene sequences, such as those suggested above with Ellen's story. You decide how to group them into chapters. If you work on the floor or wall or a big board, you can make vertical scene captions that come between the major scenes on the horizontal timeline. The story starts to have a visual shape, which, I promise you, helps you hold it in your mind.

Right now you are learning tools for evaluating and writing, and you may want to be sure of your major events before you worry about scene sequences, but it won't hurt to take a look at a chapter with this scheme in mind. It is also valuable practice to create scene sequences for chapters of a model novel.

EXERCISES

❏ Identify three major events in your model novel and observe how far apart they are in time. Now do that for your own novel. Is it possible to compress the time? What would be the effect? Or does enough necessary action happen in between the events to take up the space?

❏ Make a visual scheme (something like I did with Ellen's story) of a section from your model book. You want to go from one situation to a changed situation, identifying the steps in between. (This is the basic idea of storyboarding.) The more you do, the more you will learn. I recommend you work with at least three chapters. Don't get bogged down in the interim action; focus on the major events. Lay out the broad action of the three chapters.

Now you can enter the interim actions that take you from event to event.

Describe the pattern of the chapters.

7. Identify the most important backstory events.

By now you should know what memories hang over the story you are telling. Put them on a timeline as events: the time that such and such happened. Evaluate them, one by one, to be sure that you want them to show up in the novel. If you are going to tell a story in which you bring in whole chapters of backstory, well, in my opinion, those events are part of the foreground. You are starting *back there* even if you don't do so in the first chapter. Remember that although chronology is your best friend (you want to know things in sequence), you may not necessarily tell the story chronologically. What you do want to know is where your story really starts. What you relegate to the past should be winnowed down to a few major events. (You might leave more on the timeline than you will actually use in the novel, if knowing a denser past helps *you*.)

You have the rest of the timeline, of course, that starts with page 1, so you can consider where it is best to reveal what George did to Sarah in 1977, or why Mother, long dead, always favored her son over her daughter. As a general rule, it means more to the reader to learn about the past later rather than earlier. She has to be engaged with the protagonist's situation and needs before she cares about history. You have to resist your impulse to spill it up front. If you think history is more interesting and more important, maybe that's where you should begin the story. Maybe that is the story.

A little anecdote: A long time ago I served on a panel for the National Endowment for the Arts' creative writing prose fellowships. I read several hundred manuscripts. After about forty of them, I began a tabulation of how many introduced backstory before page 3. It was astounding. Fully two-thirds of these accomplished writers stopped action to fill in information, right at the beginning, usually on the first page or two. I thought the strategy was appropriate in about a dozen manuscripts. I tell you this to say, you have a lot of company. I would go so far as to say it is a stage of maturing as a writer to be able to wait. Just keep in mind that your first chapter is about captivating the reader in the story that is unfolding; be very wary of interrupting it to explain the past.

When you look at the progression of events on your timelines, you can see whether the past really does have the weight you thought it did, and if it does, you can make rigorous decisions about where—and why—you will tell the reader what happened. In your chain of events, do you see triggers (reminders of some kind) that bring up the past? Do you see situations where a character has reason and occasion for pondering old news? Are there lingering consequences? Has resentment or emotional fallout been simmering for decades, soon to explode? To me the classic example of Big Backstory is the horror and carnage in a family's past (abuse, murder) that explains the brother's and sister's fraught lives in Pat Conroy's *The Prince of Tides*. It's a narrative strategy that easily skids into melodrama, but it worked for Conroy.

Once you sort out the backstory you do want to include, you can study the passages where you have mentioned it—or should—and you can control:

1. The trigger (what brings it up).
2. The duration of the memory (how much page space telling it takes).
3. The nature of the emotional response (what effect remembering it has on a character).
4. The nature of new action as a result of raising the past (how the memory pushes a character into a dramatic response).

You can decide whether to include the past as an act of the character's memory (interiority) or to stop forward action to present backstory as discrete narrative. There may be several, even numerous, references to the past, whether in dialogue or in scraps of memory—ghosts of past scenes.

Don't integrate the past without making sure of three things:

1. You need to tell it.
2. This is the right time to do so.
3. It has a consequence, emotional or physical, for the character.

Every time you present the past, consider these three issues. Again, I want to emphasize that you must choose whether to tell something from the past—backstory—as part of a *present scene* (relevant to present action, brought up between characters, or in a character's interiority) or as a *flashback*—a scene or narrative summary of its own, separate from present action. There is a kind of novel that roams the past and the present like adjacent landscapes, but it takes skill to make the strategy work. Whatever you do, you don't want the reader to get confused.

Getting control of flashbacks and memories is a big part of maturing as a fiction writer, and creating a timeline (a placeholder) is a good start. You might find you want to chop some of the past right off that summary line. You might combine events—a controversial technique for memoir writers but an effective, efficient one for fiction.

A novel that uses history as the "real story" and builds the present of the novel with precision and economy is *The Piano Maker* by Kurt Palka. There are three chronologies in the book: (a) "now," when the protagonist, Helene, moves to a small village in Nova Scotia and begins working as the church pianist and choirmaster; (b) the far past, from her childhood and young adulthood in a family that made pianos through her marriage and the death of her husband in war; and (c) the near past, a horrific story of deprivation and terror in the Arctic North, which is sprung on the reader as a sudden revelation. We know Helene well—or at least see her and like her and know where she came from—before we are suddenly made aware that she did something that might be criminal. The way that Palka handles the pace of all this is worth studying. The language is measured but crisp, lyrical but subtle. Not all reviewers agreed with me, but I thought it was a brave and fascinating novel.

Decisions about what part of the story's past belong in the novel will be affected by the analysis you do in every stage of your preparations to revise. Stay fluid and don't worry. If you simply do a description of what you have in hand, that's fine.

Remember—you're writing everything down!

EXERCISES

❑ In a novel of your choice, identify an aspect of the past that impinges on the "now" of the novel.

   ▪ Is the past interesting, not a cliché?
   ▪ Does it really matter? How so?
   ▪ What effect does it have, and why now?

❑ Choose a place in your own novel where the past appears, is remembered, or in some way is relevant in the text. Evaluate (a) how it is presented (how it interrupts the flow of action) and (b) what its effect is on the story.

❑ If you have a fairly complete draft with a lot of backstory, now would be as good a time as any to do an inventory of it. Go chapter to chapter, noting where the backstory appears. Keep a list. Annotate each instance with a description of how the past is introduced and what the effect is on the present story. What you want to look for is a boring pattern or confusion or memories that don't affect what is going on at the time they are introduced. Think:

   ▪ economy
   ▪ function
   ▪ variety
   ▪ effect

8. Describe your protagonist in terms of agency, struggle, and transformation.

Nobody needs to tell you that a novel is about character. Well, sure, there are novels that aren't—the flat-out plot-flying genre and commercial books in which characters are moved along a stream of suspense and violence, driven by outside forces they have to understand and overcome (perfect examples: John Grisham's *The Firm*, Dan Brown's *The Da Vinci Code*). But the books you remember, and I hope the ones you want to write, have compelling characters. Where they come from and how you develop them—that's a subject for another book, though we certainly look at characters in your revision. You are attracted to something in a character that touches you, because character swells up out of desire and fear and need. And just as I talked about story having two forces, action and emotion, I think character has to be driven both by what is going on outside and what is roiling inside.

What I want to offer here is a scheme for talking about character development. As I've said before, many apprentice writers get trapped in stories with characters who are acted upon, the victims of events or other people who are stronger than they are. And of course we expect a character to be beset with challenges. The issue is whether the character has enough responsibility for his own fate that we empathize with his struggle; if he is defeated, we want to see that he did not go down passively; if he wins, we want him to have earned it. And if he brings about his own downfall, we appreciate reversals and consequences. Responsibility for one's own fate is a big part of making a character memorable. We expect a complex character to make some wrong decisions and bear the consequences; we expect her to face difficult choices and challenges. What thrills us is watching the character try.

AGENCY

The question, then, is: Does your protagonist have *agency*? If your novel is plot driven—let's say there are aliens invading St. Louis and your protagonist is the smartest engineer, pilot, or military mind in town—that agency will be all about responding to the threat: the hero battling outside forces. If your novel is character driven, however, it is as likely that the challenge to the protagonist will come from something she does or wants, as from something or someone outside her, and it will be something that has a cost. *Agency is the word for the character's central role in pushing the story forward.* She chooses, and acts, and bears the consequences. Maybe she fails, but not for want of trying.

My first novel, *Gringa*, was about Abilene, a young woman in Mexico during the 1968 Olympics. I know now that I was way out on a far, far limb with her as my main character, because she is tossed around by men and luck and has no real power. What I did intuitively—and I can only say it helped, not that it turned her into a heroine—was to make her stubborn, in love with the exotic, and also a bit self-deceiving. She talks herself into accepting situations that aren't good for her, but she thinks she wants them or will make the best of them; for a long time, she doesn't see that she is victimized. In the end, she does choose what is best for herself. The book ends with Abilene taking the reins of her life. She doesn't "do something" to anyone; her movement into agency is her retreat from the context in which she was abused. Ultimately, I think the novel was as much about the setting as it was about Abilene. Place was a crucible for her growth, as the novel was for my own.

Agency doesn't mean cops with guns, cowboys with horses, or biceps as big as thighs. It means a character who pushes himself. Of course a character can do the wrong thing. Emma Bovary displayed plenty of agency, but her rosary of bad choices led her to her deathbed. Sometimes what a character wants is wrong, but following the desire of that character mesmerizes the reader. Here, I am thinking of Anna Karenina. The reader knows Anna should turn away from Vronsky, but the pull of her desire is greater than good sense, and that is why her fate moves us so much.

Sometimes agency may not seem possible. In *When the Emperor Was Divine*, a Japanese American family is sent to a camp for the duration of the war. What kind of agency could they possibly have? They could do their best to take care of themselves, their health and family ties. They could maintain belief in their integrity and the future. They could survive to rebuild their lives.

Sometimes you will have characters who try to exercise agency and it is not possible for them to prevent their defeat. In those stories, the struggle *is* the story. (Think of *The Old Man and the Sea* or the protagonists of Jim Harrison's novellas in *Legends of the Fall*.)

If you are writing about someone with little power, possibly someone who will fail to achieve what she wants, be sure you illustrate that agency is about a person's drive to act. It is possible to lack power but at the same time to be fiercely active in a struggle to achieve it. The act of deliberate struggle (as opposed to flailing when attacked) is a sign of agency. In Dai Sijie's charming novel *Balzac and the Little Chinese Seamstress*, two boys are sent to the countryside for reeducation during China's Cultural Revolution. The boys "win" because they come upon a cache of books and discover the power of stories. The struggle and the victory are inside their heads and hearts. They don't fight Mao, but in a fabulist way, Mao loses.

In *The Piano Maker*, Helene has no real power, but she is a strong woman and morally capable of defending herself. One of the most interesting and effective things about the novel is that the author establishes Helene's new life in the Nova Scotia village, building for her a community, before her peaceful life there is shattered. The goodwill that she has built up, simply by being her true self, contributes to her agency when her freedom is threatened. It's a generous vision, that a good person is one who behaves as a good person, and knows she has done so; and that such a person should not be punished for the cruelties of fate.

Think of how your character's choices move the story along. And, as you begin the process of revision, see if you can strengthen the character's will, wit, and wisdom.

STRUGGLE AND TRANSFORMATION

Of course you aren't going to write a novel about someone who gets what she wants at the beginning. There has to be a struggle that injures or denies the protagonist his desire, upsets the equilibrium of his situation, or puts people he loves at risk. There has to be a tug-of-war.

There should be two levels of struggle:

1. The need for something concrete that the protagonist is fighting to get (such as safe haven, a scholarship at ballet school, or the love of a partner).
2. The urgent desire to be better.

Just think of all the questions raised by those two desires! Is the thing the protagonist wants achievable? Would it be good for him? Does he truly understand what it would be? Who else wants it? How does the protagonist define "being good" and "doing good"? Is he realistic about the sacrifice something may demand? These are the kinds of questions that help you complicate plot. *What if?*

Always, I pose questions because in answering them you may find a new plot point, a new aspect of character, an idea for a detail that makes a scene work better.

I do like to think of a novel as the journey of a person trying to be a better person. If that sounds a bit pat, think of it this way: You get to define the journey and all the challenges along its way, and you get to define what "good" means, and how far from that state the character is at the beginning. One way or another, it has to be hard for the protagonist to get from beginning to end. And it has to be worth the struggle.

The quality of the protagonist's goal, the tenor of the protagonist's struggle to achieve it, and the satisfaction that comes with arrival all create transformation. A character can fail and still become a better person, just as a character can achieve or attain but discover he has lost himself.

One of the strongest—and most unlikely—heroes of a recent novel is Christopher John Francis Boone, a mildly autistic and mathematically gifted adolescent boy who sets out to solve a murder—of a neighbor's dog—and learns that he is capable of far more than solving intricate puzzles. *The Curious Incident of the Dog in the Night-Time* won millions of readers who followed Christopher's clever investigation and his transformation into a more independent person. You could learn a lot about character development by walking through this plot, listing each challenge and his strategy for meeting it. Everything is about action, because the boy's emotional state is static. (Or so we are told.) The way a dog's death leads to a restructured family is a marvel of plotting. Yet the very nature of Christopher's syndrome is that he doesn't change and doesn't want to. How, then, is he a protagonist? How does he work for something he wants? The clever conceit of the novel is that Christopher admires mystery stories, where questions are solved by finding and examining clues that solve the puzzle. He has clear goals.

Of course there are stories about characters who can't or won't change. Heathcliff's malevolent passion never changes, and Cathy is never able to resist, but oh what a struggle! The strength of intransigence, wreaking havoc, is appealing if it is done with great dramatic power.

If you can describe your character in these terms—agency, struggle, and transformation—you can "test" your plot points against your definitions, and you can assess the depth of character development by how dramatic these elements are. Ultimately, you have to define agency for yourself and your characters, and from that perspective, construct the struggle that is the main thread of your story.

How much power does your protagonist have in the beginning? Does she lose or gain power in the story? When? How?

What does the character want? Why doesn't she already have it? How hard is it to get it? Does someone else want it, too, providing competition, or is it that someone doesn't think the character should have it?

And if the character does achieve her desire, or if she doesn't—how does the struggle change her? How does it change her relationships?

Exercises

- ❏ Find a place in the novel where your character acts with fierce intention.
- ❏ Find a place where it seems impossible that she will solve a problem that threatens her happiness—or the happiness of someone she loves.
- ❏ Find a place where she behaves in a way she wouldn't have chosen to behave, or been able to, in the beginning (like Christopher, the teenager mentioned above, who sets out on a train ride to London, a miracle of independent endeavor).

If you don't have such character turns in your novel yet, is it possible to create them?

9. Describe your protagonist's fate and its relationship to your vision.

Resolution

At this point, describe how your novel ends—how it leaves the protagonist. Was the struggle successful? Were important lessons learned? What was lost or won? Was there surprise and satisfaction in the story's resolution? Think again about your statement of the story's vision—how things work in the world of the novel, what is inevitable, who has power. Look back at the situation the character was in when the story problem was established. What situation is the character in at the end? How do you leave the reader? Keep in mind that the best kind of ending for a novel is one that feels both inevitable and surprising. You want the reader to recognize that this is exactly how things had to be, but you don't want the reader to think: Well, I knew that would happen. The tension should not be broken prematurely. Ending a story in a way that isn't predictable is a big challenge, maybe one of the hardest in writing a novel. If you've had trouble finding that ending, keep thinking, *What if?* Finding a more satisfying ending may take you back into the meat of the story, but that's revising!

Ask yourself: At the end of my novel, has the life of the protagonist been opened or closed? I'm not talking about life or death, I'm talking about the possibility for happiness. Was this where the protagonist was always headed? Was it because of a flaw or a strength of character? Or was it because the world of the story was so powerful an influence? The answer lies in the convergence of your vision of the world of the novel with your character's agency. And keep in mind that when the reader leaves that last page, she is saying good-bye to someone she has been with for many hours. You want it to be hard to leave the character, because he means something to the reader now. And yet you want that sense of perfect closure.

Can you go back and identify points in the story where the choices your character made put him closer to this particular ending? And even if the reader then thinks, I knew this would happen, there has to have been the possibility that it would not. The best response isn't: I knew that was coming. It is, rather: Of course! I should have seen that coming.

TITLE

Now think about the title. Write it down. I bring it up now because I think it is so related to the character and the theme of the novel. What element of meaning does it reflect? Setting? Fate? Relationships? Events? A character's name? A good title beckons the reader, of course, but to my mind it does far more—it establishes an expectation, however subliminally, that will be met by something that is unique about the story. Consider a few:

Madame Bovary. Now, you may say, that's the name of the main character, so what? Ah, so true; but notice that it isn't *Emma* Bovary. It is the woman trapped in her loveless marriage, the spiral of her bad choices, her suffocating life, her fate. *Wife*.

The Great Gatsby. Like so many good titles, this one is ironic. Gatsby had a lot going for him but he overreached. He was great at self-invention.

The Grapes of Wrath. The story goes that John Steinbeck's wife came up with this title, which carries so much weight with its biblical reference (the Book of Revelation). Even more directly, it is pulled from the abolitionist anthem "The Battle Hymn of the Republic." Steinbeck was writing his great story of the oppression of the poor by the selfish landowners and banks. His title is testimony of his commitment to justice, and his ire when the poor are trampled.

For Whom the Bell Tolls. Again, a reference ("it tolls for thee") that strikes a chord. Again, Hemingway plowing the fields of war. This is a title of fate and vision, poetry and sorrow.

A Tree Grows in Brooklyn. This wonderful classic coming-of-age novel is all about place and time, and the title captures that, while also calling up the idea of a young person coming of age.

Waiting for the Barbarians. Again, a title of context, South Africa at its cruelest time. You have to know things aren't going to work out well.

The Good Mother. Sad to say how ironic this. Sue Miller's heroine is a mother who loves her child like breath itself, but she is punished for being a woman; the child is taken away from her.

Make a list of novels you admire and figure out how each title relates to the concepts you've been reading about. It's never easy to come up with exactly the right phrase, but don't give up too soon. You want your title to lure the reader and promise exactly what you deliver. Make a game of it—try to match a title to each of the categories I listed: vision, premise, world of the story, setting, context, character.

EXERCISES

- ❑ List three novels you admire. Describe the protagonist's *fate* in each one. Consider the emotional effect of a character's fate on you, the reader.
- ❑ Write a new last sentence for your novel that somehow represents a sense of the character's fate. Try several.
- ❑ Make a list of books you like. Describe what each title says about the book. Try to make up alternative titles.

10. Describe your other major characters.

In a first draft you may have characters who don't really need to be there, or ones whose functions aren't well developed. You may have characters who are in their own right interesting, but who don't create push and pull with the protagonist. You know, of course, that the antagonist—the character most in conflict with the protagonist—will have to be strong enough to exacerbate the protagonist's struggle. But every character has to relate to the protagonist in a way that matters. Lots of novels have minor characters whose function seems to be to make the story lively or shocking, but the need to decorate your story isn't a reason to add a character. If you have someone in your story who could be taken out without upsetting the progress of events or the structure of the story, you have to question whether you need the character at all. (I'm not referring to the drive-by characters who function as part of a setting, such as clerks at stores, taxi drivers, musicians at a concert, etc.) There are of course stories that require numerous walk-on or recurring minor characters. Alan Furst's spy novels set in Germany in the Second World War are remarkable for this very quality;

everyone from waiters to military officers is distinct and colorful, adding both to the plot (what is coming) and the context (Nazi Germany).

Julie Otsuka's *When the Emperor Was Divine* includes numerous minor characters who need to be there for the story to proceed, but whose function does not require elaboration. For example: a storekeeper; people on the train when the family is going to the camp; guards. But a minor character can be memorable, such as the man who is shot at the camp's fence; he represents the terrible effect of deprivation and hopelessness on some prisoners. The novel is interesting in that there are no major antagonists. The family is in conflict with a system created by the government out of suspicion and fear.

Here is a brief example, from *Walking Dunes*, of a minor character who doesn't take up a lot of page space but is important to the story. Sissy is a girl who lives off the same alley as David, and basically, that's their relationship. But she looks up to him and catches him to talk now and then. She is a troubled girl whose efforts to hook up with a popular boy are undermining her fragile mental health. She keeps a notebook, and she gives it to David for safekeeping. (She doesn't want her parents to see it.) Later, when she is killed, the notebook is important because it shows her state of mind and it backs up the assertions of the boy who shot her.

How does Sissy reflect on David's character and create a problem for him?

Sissy is a lonely girl who wants someone to love her. She has been trying to win the affections of a popular boy. She sees David as a friend, even though she really has no reason to.

Sissy, like David, is a poor kid wanting something better, but she lacks his talent.

Sissy thinks of David as an ally, but to David she is just the neighbor girl.

Sissy is important because the aftermath of her death
provides an ethical challenge to David, who has the
girl's notebook and knows that she asked David's friend
to help her die. (The boy shot her with her father's rifle.)
Where David is ambitious and in some ways ruthless,
wanting desperately to climb out of his poverty, Sissy is
trapped in her belief that life has nothing to give her.
David knows that Sissy has been raped. He has ignored
the fact, and her. David doesn't give Sissy's notebook to
the attorney who should have it because he doesn't
want to be in any way attached to her; she is pitiful
and he is afraid he'll be drawn into a scandal. So Sissy
is a foil that shows David's moral weakness (even
though it turns out the notebook would never have
been used).

The girls in the novel project different aspects of David's
character. Sissy is minor except that her need exposes his shal-
lowness and cowardice, most important, to himself. Glee is a
cheerleader, a pretty girl who is crazy about him, and he never
really sees her as a person with her own desires—other than for
him. Patsy is the morally strongest character in the book, another girl in David's neighborhood and class. She wants to be
an artist of some kind, perhaps an actress; she wants to have a
vibrant, fulfilling life, and she intends to leave Basin, Texas, to
pursue it, however hard she has to strive. David loves talking to
her and being drawn into her dreams and her sensibility, but
she contrasts with him in the kind of agency she is creating for
herself. Although he is attracted to Patsy, he has attached himself to the beautiful daughter of a wealthy family, seeing her as
his way out of Basin, even though deep down he thinks the girl
is vapid.

When you look at your lists of characters, take the time to
pair each with the protagonist and consider the function of the
character—what she or he does to move the story along—and

how the character provokes or reveals something about your protagonist. Think about how each character also has his own story problem. Does that problem intersect or parallel the protagonist's story problem? *This is a subplot.*

All major characters have to have a reason to be in the protagonist's story; at the same time, they have to have stories of their own. Finding intersections is how you build conflict or alliance.

How large is the cast of your story? Are there characters who duplicate one another's functions? Would an additional minor character add color and perhaps a thread to the plot? Is everybody the same age for a reason? On a large piece of paper, draw stick figures or circles and label your main characters. Draw lines of connection, arrows of conflict, arcs of love. Look for ways to tighten and heighten relationships. See if one character could "do the work" of two. Look for characters who are too much alike.

EXERCISES

These exercises are challenging. *Don't rush them.*

- ❑ In a novel of your choice, list the major characters. For each one other than the protagonist, state why that character is important to the story. For each character, consider what story he or she has, and how it intersects the protagonist's story. Describe two or three events connected to the character; are they independent of the protagonist, or do they intersect the main plotline?
- ❑ Choose a character other than your protagonist and answer these questions:
  1. What situation is the character in at the beginning of the story?
  2. How does the situation create a problem (and a question) for the character?

3. How does the character's situation and/or problem intersect with one of the protagonist's?
4. Is the character an antagonist or an ally?
5. Is the character fundamental to the plot? (Could another character assume the particular actions of this one?)
6. How does the nature and behavior of this character contrast with the protagonist's?

❑ Go through your chapters, listing every character. This is a good activity to do on a large sheet of paper so that you can see everything at once. Make three or four columns for your list. You want to be able to look across the lists to see names recurring. If the task seems too formidable, do it first with a single chapter. Then do it with a section of the book that has an arc—the beginning that sets everything up and starts the conflict, perhaps. If it still feels difficult, do the exercise first with a short published novel that you know and like. Then go back to your manuscript.

List your major characters in caps. (The story has to have the character for events to occur; the character is part of the obligatory story. This list will include the characters who are important in subplots.)

Now list minor ones in small letters. (The character serves a need in a scene but appears briefly, or in a way that moves the action in a small way.) Don't include people like doormen, taxi drivers, store clerks, etc., who are more part of the setting than characters. If they don't affect the plot, they don't go on your list. But minor characters can be important ones. For example, in *The Last Painting of Sara de Vos*, there is a private detective who makes an important discovery, but he appears only once, albeit for a lengthy scene. There is a conservation scientist (a person who tests for the authenticity of a painting) who appears twice briefly, but is important because what she learns provides a twist in the plot. On the other hand, there are a couple of characters in the first scene who never appear again; I wouldn't put them on my list.

Annotate each character's name with a phrase or label. If it is clear to you that a character is part of a subplot—a separate (intersecting or parallel) story line—note that. You will come back to him when you work with "threads" later on.

And remember that characters are not only themselves; they are also projections and antagonists of the main character. Foils. Modifiers. Mirrors. They represent currents of subtext, setting up triangle love patterns, struggles for money and authority, the weight of the past, etc. A subplot is both a *who* and a *what*. Save the list; you will need it later.

Look over your list:

Who acts to undermine the protagonist's goal?

Who acts to support the protagonist?

Are there any triangles? (Two people opposing the third?)

Which characters are most present (appear in the most chapters)? Are they interesting? (Memorable?)

What secrets are in the subplots? What happens when they are revealed?

Are there characters that really, truly don't need to be there? Don't choke your plot with extraneous story lines.

❑ Find a scene that you think is one of the most dramatic events in the novel. Who (other than your protagonist) is important in the scene? Does this character appear often in the novel? If this is a single appearance, is it an important one? Could the function be folded into another character? Repeat this exercise with other dramatic events.

What you are doing now is bringing all the actors on the stage so you have a picture of the whole cast in mind. Come back to it again. You have been looking at the connections between characters, and the ways that they bump against one another.

Now think about each character *as an interesting invention*. Could any character be more colorful, scary, appealing, mysterious? Are any two characters too much alike in appearance or behavior? Conversely, is anyone "over the top," too broadly drawn in comparison to other characters or to the tone of the novel?

Assessment

How have I told my story?

1. Describe your point of view and how it works.
2. Describe the structure of your novel.
3. Write a tagline for each chapter—the list is a summary of your story.
4. Evaluate your first chapter.
5. Choose six noncontiguous scenes and describe how they connect across the plot.
6. Mark the scenes to indicate backstory. Evaluate for relevance, economy, trigger, and transition.
7. Mark passages of summary and exposition, and evaluate.
8. Mark passages of interiority, and evaluate.
9. Choose two key scenes and evaluate them using a scene template.

As you begin to evaluate what you have written, keep good notes. If you have a bound copy, you can write on the blank pages when you are assessing particular scenes or chapters. Or start a separate notebook or log in which you record your observations and possible revision issues. You want to compile a picture of your draft that allows you to make decisions down the line about what needs to be done. It's impossible to ski through a manuscript and keep everything in your head.

1. Describe your point of view and how it works.

When you started writing your novel, chances are you used a default point of view, by which I mean the sound of someone telling the story "came to you" as you began the work. It's how you heard the story in your head. That's fine, except that you want to consider if it is the most effective approach.

Some think of point of view in simple terms of person: first ("I" or even "we"), second ("you"), or third ("he" or "she"). You probably already sense that the decision about what POV to use is not that simple. There are considerations of distance, intimacy, voice, authority, and more. You can write a thesis on the subject, but ultimately the choice of POV is first intuitive, and then considered.

Here's the simplest way to think of it: *A narrator is telling a story.* The story concerns events and the characters who are part of those events. A particular character or certain characters are most affected by the events and have the most participation in them, so we are especially interested in what they think and how they feel, though it can also be very effective to have an onlooker tell a story. You choose where to "stand" in relation to the story. Is the narrator an observer or someone in the thick of it?

I find it helpful to consider these elements of point of view:

Whose consciousness are we hearing?
How close are we to the story (in time, in intimacy)?
Is there commentary?

The first question could be answered most simply by naming the main character and using third person. This is the most common strategy and there is nothing wrong with it. But you have a world of choices. One of my students is writing a fascinating novel in which a house sometimes comments on its occupants. We had a novel lately with a dog's perspective. In an omniscient (see all, know all) POV, the consciousness is the narrator, a kind of overarching angel of the story. Flaubert uses this kind of voice in *Madame Bovary*, but he also shifts voice (the sound of the telling) to reveal what Emma Bovary is thinking, changing diction to reflect her perception and attitude. (This was an innovation; it's hard to think there was a time when writers didn't use "free indirect discourse.")

The second question about distance has a whole lot to do with the voice. Is the narration looking back on something in the near past, or to the distant past? Is there an "occasion" for the telling, something that has called up memory? (A death? The reappearance of someone? The discovery of an artifact?) Is the story being discovered in the course of the narration, or revealed by someone who knows it? Nick Carraway is telling Gatsby's story after it happened. He expresses his view of himself as the author—a person trying to find the meaning of what has happened. So he *was* close to the action (close enough to be an observer), but, in telling, he has stepped back and *is* reflecting.

Conversely, in *The Curious Incident of the Dog in the Night-Time* the narrator is a boy who is charmingly direct in describing not only what he does as he goes about investigating a dog's death, but also explaining to the reader why he does things his special way, without any conventional perspective—that is, distance—at all.

Most of my students have come to me using the close-third-person POV. This means "entering the head" of the character and experiencing everything as that character acts, sees, and feels. For many years it seemed to me most American short stories were written in this POV, and many novels, but I see more variety now. Writers from other cultures have never been locked into our ideas about point of view.

At its most confining, the close-third-person POV means that you are hamstrung by the one perspective, so you can't tell what is happening if that character isn't observing what you want to reveal. *If your choice of POV strangles your ability to tell the story, you need to revisit your decision.* The main thing I tell my students is that if you want to stick to your protagonist's point of view, it doesn't mean your text should sound like the protagonist would speak. If you want to use the protagonist's voice, use first person.

In a novel with multiple main characters, the switch is made in a kind of rotation, and you are more likely to use this whirling POV if a single one has you up a tree. Usually it's an alternation of close third views about events and people closely aligned, but increasingly, innovative writers are varying multiple aspects of story, sometimes contrasting perspectives across generations or populations.

I've also noticed lately that writers are starting to be quite bold in moving around the point of view in their novels. Within the same chapter, often within the same scene, more than one character thinks about what is going on. Novels I've recently read that do this, I would say successfully: Emma Straub, *The Vacationers*; Nancy Clark, *The Hills at Home*; Meg Mitchell Moore, *The Arrivals.* I'm sure there'll be lots more. I think it's all part of a growing awareness that a story is an object that is being observed by a narrator who knows what people are thinking and feeling. It's a matter of deciding where you want your narrator to stand and what you want her to reveal.

You can choose to be mostly in the consciousness of the main character, in a third-person POV, but I prefer to think of this as the voice of the novel (its narration) *observing the character thinking,* just as it observes the actions. You can still stick with that character (not go inside other characters' thinking; not tell things happening if the character isn't present), but the rigidity of "being inside the head" relaxes. It is possible to give the reader information that the character would know but isn't necessarily thinking about at the moment. It is possible to remark on the character's behavior or feelings. If you are integrating a lot of backstory into the narration, you just about have to do this, unless you are going to say, over and over, "she remembered." ("Remembering" matters if a character is ruminating, regretting, analyzing, etc. It isn't effective if it's just an excuse to present information.)

I urge apprentice writers to do some practice writing using an objective dramatic POV. Tell the story using dialogue and description, with no interiority. Tell what you are seeing and hearing. It has worked for Cormac McCarthy, Elmore Leonard, and Ernest Hemingway, among others. This approach forces you to let action be strong and clear enough for the reader to interpret, without a character's thoughts, and it can break sloppy habits of the character inserting remarks about everything. You don't have to pledge lifelong allegiance to it.

If, however, you want to maintain the closeness of the character's perspective, you have to consider whether third person or first person is best. Both have the same constraint—you can tell only what the character knows—but in first person the reader accepts more commentary as natural, whereas describing what a character is thinking all the time can get distracting, even annoying. In the case of first person, you must ask what reason a narrator would have to be telling the story. Are we, the readers, meant to feel that we are present in the action or that we are hearing about it (consequences and all)?

An author often chooses first person to tell a tale about something that happened long ago about which perspective has been gained—or can be gained by the telling. I find this the most natural use of first person, perhaps because I associate it with an ancient sense of storytelling rather than a modern "here I am and it's going on now" sensibility. In Joseph Conrad's *Lord Jim*, for example, the character Marlow struggles to tell the story of a man named Jim.

In a story that casts its view back, there may be a tone of regret or shame or the pleasure of finally recognizing meaning about long-ago occurrences. Wendell Berry's novel *Hannah*

Coulter is told in the voice of a woman looking back on a lifetime in her Kentucky farming community, in a cadence that is both common and poetic—characteristic of Berry's storytelling.

Marilynne Robinson makes interesting use of first person in *Gilead*, when elderly John Ames writes a letter to his seven-year-old son, revealing the long history of his family, his friendships, and his own journey of faith. She also creates tension in unusual ways—with ideas as much as feelings; this is a man wrestling with his sense of guilt, and with his faith. Because of her conceit of the letter, it is natural for the character, John Ames, to fill pages with commentary: his regrets, his joys, his fears.

Both close first and close third should be considered in terms of tense, as well; some writers like the present tense for its immediacy. It says *this is happening*, rather than *this is what happened*. I think it's hard to control this strategy, and it is confining, almost claustrophobic, if used inexpertly. It also creates tension with the notion that a story told is a story whose meaning has been considered. But if it feels natural to you, you can use it and assess whether it proved useful.

Most apprentice writers would expect that a first-person narrator would remark on history and events, character and feelings, but they might not consider that commentary used to be usual in third-person POV stories, too. We don't see many omniscient narrators anymore (those who know everything, see everything, and therefore can tell everything), but if you give yourself a little more distance from that close third person, you may find it possible to say things that wouldn't fit otherwise.

If you are up for a study of POV that allows the narrative to remark on characters' behavior subtly but with great effect, I can't think of a better model than Alice Munro. Go through any of her stories and mark out the places where she says *what a character is like, how the character sees the world, what the character's behavior tells about her*. Munro manages to be inside and outside of characters at the same time.

Note that I have referred to the "voice" of the story or the "voice" of narration. *The "narrator" is the* something, *not quite a* someone *telling the story.* As if stories come from heaven, or history, or fate. What you want to strive for is a kind of falling into that voice, that isn't quite you (you are the author) and isn't quite the character. It is the story telling itself. It is magic.

EXAMPLES

The possibilities are dizzying, and this may be your first time out as a novelist. Remember that a story doesn't have to be fancy to be effective. It's more important to be clear, engaging, and comfortable with narration. When novelists use innovative strategies to tell their stories, I believe it is because that is how they hear the story; the complexities are part of their story.

Let's look at a couple of simple examples that demonstrate, I believe, that a straightforward third person is flexible and more spacious than you may think. You won't stop and think: How clever this novelist is! Instead, you'll follow the story with enjoyment. I just read Donna Leon's latest novel of Venice, *The Waters of Eternal Youth.* Her novels have an accessible structure you could study as a model. She narrates from the point of view of Commissario Guido Brunetti, an intellectual, compassionate, curious, and competent police inspector, a man with a warm family life and a love of his city, despite its many social and physical flaws. Her writing is accomplished but it isn't complicated or fancy. You can see what she is doing. Here's how I describe her POV:

Leon tells a story, filling in history and background, bringing in new information and events, while following the movements of the inspector as he goes about his work and his life. Intermittently, the protagonist remarks on what is happening, sometimes processing it as an investigator, but he also often has philosophical reactions, expressing himself in a way that makes him the insightful and empathetic character so many readers enjoy. At other times Leon *observes* what Brunetti thinks. I'll begin with an example of that, as Brunetti discusses a murder victim with a barman who knew him:

> "Did he work?" Brunetti asked, aware that his professional responsibility was to check other possible motives for Cavanis' murder and not only his long-ago act of courage.

Later, on that same page, Leon describes a moment's interaction between Brunetti and his partner Vianello. Note that she is describing the interaction, of which Brunetti is a part, but without being "in his head":

> Vianello and Brunetti exchanged a brief glance. Neither spoke, each waiting for the other to do it.

An apprentice writer, struggling to maintain a close-third-person perspective, might have ended up with something like this instead:

> Brunetti exchanged a brief glance with Vianello. Vianello didn't speak, and neither did Brunetti, as he was waiting for Vianello to speak first.

It isn't necessary to be so tight.
There are, however, interior comments, such as:

> Brunetti told himself, but did not say aloud, that Manuela might not be the only one who was brain damaged.

I am especially fond of the inspector's musings—he is a reader of classics, while his formidable wife, Paola, is a professor of American literature. Here is an example:

Brunetti found himself thinking of Dante's belief that heresy was a form of intellectual stubbornness, the refusal to abandon a mistaken idea. In Dante's case, this path led to eternal damnation; in his own case, Brunetti reflected, intellectual stubbornness might well be leading him deep into the Dark Wood of Error.

I especially want to make the point that a close POV doesn't keep the narration from giving history and commentary. It requires little or no tags of "she thought," "he knew," etc. Here is a passage from my novel *Beyond Deserving*. The occasion is the fiftieth wedding anniversary party for the parents of twin sons whose wives are POV characters. This excerpt is from Ursula's perspective. Her daughter, Juliette, dances to the music of two violins.

Juliette begins to dance. At first she takes only a small space. She moves, almost like the musicians, in a flutter. Then her arms move out from her like a flower unfolding. Her head rises and her face, sweet and pale, is sad and yearning. She turns gently, once, and again, venturing out away from the music, into the center of the hall. Her arms wind up and pull her heavenward, beyond the building, away from their quarrels . . .

For fifty years the Fishers have been saying wrong things, or nothing at all, or pretending to talk while they speak riddles and small deceits. Here, though, is a Fisher who with a few deft moves has rescued them from a day's spite . . .

All of this is observed by Ursula, but it is *told by the narrator*, in the *diction of narration*, and not in Ursula's voice. We aren't interrupted with "she thought" and a tangle of syntax. Ursula is present, observing, *but the narrator tells*.

If you are a lover of popular women's fiction (Elizabeth Berg, Joanna Trollope, Sara Gruen, Kristin Hannah, etc.) and you want to write it, you will want to study how POV is used to establish intimacy and tension. Find passages and use them as models; ask, *What is the structure of this passage?* followed by your own writing in the same general style. Note, too, that these successful writers don't ply with a tired old oar. They write fresh, imaginative, intelligent stories.

One writer who has made a successful career expertly employing the intimacy of close POV is Jodi Picoult, whose novels explore issues in the culture, and always make them personal and affecting. In *The Storyteller*, she tells of the unlikely friendship of a young woman and an old man, a survivor of the Second World War who turns out to have worked at Auschwitz. Her writing is full of the narrator's observations and opinions, all nested in ample description, action, and dialogue. Some chapters are busy with the daily stuff of present-day life. Other chapters are rich narration about the past. We always know where we are and what it is like there. We always know how the narrator feels, but in a context—her own history, the old man's history, stories of war, family, courage, atrocity. When she switches perspective to that of a narrator relaying the experiences of war, she completely changes the tone and rhythm of the prose, with very little dialogue. The contrast between the voices is controlled and effective. If you read one of her books, try to figure out why she approaches different parts of the story in the perspectives she uses. Assume she made choices based on the subject matter and the effect she wanted to have on the reader.

I'm aware that I have made several references to women's fiction, and this is because this "genre" is characterized by emotional interiority and usually uses a close POV. We see next to none of that in popular novels preferred by male readers, where the plot is paramount and sentiment is spare. However, I think best-selling author Michael Connelly's novels about the troubled detective Harry Bosch deftly balance plot with character-centered story. He always has a burden on his conscience. Philip Kerr, too, creates a protagonist whose life is a constant engagement with threat, but whose intelligence and sensitivity are drawn deftly with interior reflection. In this he is much like another novelist of World War II–era Europe, Alan Furst. Both are impressive historical fiction writers.

So WHAT ARE the rules for point of view? It comes down to this: Find a way to tell your story that feels natural to you and that allows you to find the balance of event and reflection that keeps the story moving while also deepening the engagement of the reader with the fate of the characters. If you vary the perspective (switch POV), do so deliberately. You may find yourself slipping into a change. That's fine. Write a while, and then stop to read and think about the switch. Is there a pattern to the variety? What are you accomplishing by changing perspective? Try what feels right. Follow your impulse, give it a fair try, and think about the overall effect in revision. It's important to "teach" the reader what POV you are using right away, rather than springing a change on her.

Read your work aloud often; you will hear if it is awkward. If you don't stumble in reading what you wrote, you probably didn't stumble in writing it. The main question to ask as you review the text: *Is there any place a reader might be confused?*

Most of all, read and study how other writers do it. I think you will be amazed at the variety of approaches, and the freedom open to you.

Have you early on established your point of view—even if it means that it shifts—so that the reader isn't confused? And if you are using a shifting POV, is that established early on?

Does your point of view help you convey your vision of the story world?

Are you comfortable with the POV? (You can't sustain a voice that feels strained.)

Do you like the sound of the voice? (Read it aloud!)

AN UNCONVENTIONAL STRUCTURE

I'm going to talk briefly about point of view in a novel of mine, *More Than Allies*. I choose it because although it is a short novel with a simple plot, the POV design was challenging. I knew I was going to alternate the perspective of two young mothers in a small Oregon town who, because of some trouble their sons get into, become allies. I wanted to present their lives, at first separately, and then when they are together near the end of the book. I wanted to give them voice mostly by showing what their lives consist of. Both are poor but hardworking. Both are motherless, and they worry about their own parenting skills. Both are separated from their husbands, men who have matured and want to put their families back together. And both have deep interior lives—the histories and feelings people don't guess when they see them. A Mexican maid. A substitute teacher, once a foster child. A couple of moms.

At the same time, I didn't want to interrupt my main strategy, which emphasized scenes, by interrupting action with backstory and musing. I felt all boxed in by my first draft (which was already a revision of a "finished" manuscript in which both women had appeared as minor characters). And then I thought, I'll just do what feels right and see if it works. I'll ignore all the advice I've read about sticking to my POV guns. I soon realized that what I wanted to do in POV was intertwined with what I had to structurally.

So here are some observations of the book's structure.

1. There is a kind of prologue and also a kind of epilogue, but in fact they are the same event—the car journey the women and their sons make from Oregon to Texas to reunite with their husbands/fathers. The first passage is when they are leaving Oregon; the second passage is when they are arriving in Texas. This is in June 1992.

The passages are told by Maggie and are concerned with how she feels about Dulcie. They probably will never see one another again, but their friendship is enshrined in Maggie's tribute to it. So there is first-person commentary.

2. Maggie and Dulcie alternate third-person POV—not in a rigid structure. This is the ongoing "present" of the story. The emphasis is on scenes.

3. There are short texts, like interleafs. They present short scenes from the past, such as a time when Maggie was with Mo before they were married. Then a time when she was fourteen and she revisited the town where she had once lived, and where her mother later died.

4. Dulcie is seen by Maggie as wise. She tells Maggie about her dreams, and there are passages in which Maggie thinks about what Dulcie has said. There is also a passage about Dulcie and her dreams from her own POV. These passages are italicized and each would be one of the "interleafs."

5. There is a flashback to Maggie's mother's death, another interleaf.

6. There are letters from the absent husbands. (Italicized interleaf.)

I think my small innovations fit the story perfectly. I don't present these examples as models so much as to make my case that if you let go of your fear of POV, you may find ways to let it serve your story better. Also, you can see that how you present character perspective is tied with how you structure the novel. There is a world of invention and strategy in the ways writers utilize point of view, but by far the most usual way is straightforward and uncomplicated.

The only real rule in writing a novel is to keep the reader engaged.

EXERCISES

❑ Choose a novel that uses the point of view you are using. Study the first chapter, looking at how that point of view is established, and how it works. Consider another way the story could have been told. (Could something be told that can't in the present perspective? What would be lost?)

The more novels you study, the more comfortable you will be in making choices about your own writing.

❑ Describe your point of view in these terms:

Whose consciousness are we in? Are the thoughts of the character revealed *as they are being thought by the character*? Or are they "observed" by the narration?

How close are we to the story? Did it take place a long time ago? Is it taking place "as we read it"? Is there a tone of looking back, or looking on?

Does the narration comment on the action, other than what the character is thinking?

2. Describe the structure of your novel.

Plot is the arrangement of events in a logical pattern that shapes the events of a story. It is usually thought of as having a "mainline" stream of events (the plot) and secondary lines (subplots).

Let's clarify what the difference is between a *plot* and a *subplot*. The plot is the stream of action we care most about, the one with the question that must be answered. It is about the protagonist. If that's all you have, you have a very thin novel. You need subplots to complement and complicate the plot and to make the story world rich and intriguing.

Subplots are plots of their own—each one also has a question to answer, and a sequence of actions leading to some kind of satisfaction of the question. It's possible to have a protagonist-centered subplot (something else going on), but often they center around other characters. Subplots don't matter as much as the plot; they don't take up as much space on the page; they aren't as complicated—but you need them. In fact, subplots should complicate the main plot, feed it, intersect with it, and be resolved in a way that also resolves aspects of the main story. A subplot usually starts later than the main plot, but often ends at about the same time, though it can be resolved sooner. The more your multiple resolutions relate to one another, though, the better.

Some subplots may involve people and questions not related to the main plot. They keep the novel from moving like a runaway train. They make the protagonist's life more "real." They provide sidebar information, action, and relationships. You don't want them to be neat lines of action that could be deleted without affecting the main story, however. Plot and subplot have to intersect in some ways, if only by the protagonist being in both. I think it's easy to grasp the idea of subplots if you think of TV shows that switch around among characters and events. So let's take *Blue Bloods*, with Tom Selleck as Frank Reagan, New York City's police commissioner. He always has some kind of ethical issue he has to work out (subplot). Two of his sons are cops and his daughter is a prosecutor. Each of them always has a story, too, and one has to deal with the primary question of the episode—how will they catch the criminal? (plot)—while the other two deal with problems that may be related to the main story or may be separate, less complicated concerns (subplots). The whole family comes together for dinner near the end of the show, and much of what has happened is hashed out. This all sounds simplistic, and it is, because it's a formula. In a novel, you want to create your own formula, and you have time to make it resonate more deeply, and to make the complications take longer to be resolved. But the idea of Plot A going on, while B, C, and D intersect or parallel it, is the most familiar recipe for story we have in commercial novels. Good novels don't put it on a plate so simply, of course. But if you are having problems with your plot, try reducing the elements as much as possible and then building on the simple structure. I have students invent stories like these in short workshop sessions and toss them out to one another like balls on the playground.

The best way to keep control of your subplots is to make lists of the steps in each one—a list of scenes that belong to that line of the story. When does it start? When does it end? How does it intersect, shadow, or illuminate the main plotline? Do the same work for your subplots that you do for your central plotline: Assess their aboutness (in relation to the main story, of course). Create sequences that have rising action, moments of pressure and release, and so on.

I'm not going to discuss craft issues associated with multiple-main-plotline novels, except to say that they are hard to control. Approaches that alternate voices or plots can be annoying instead of intriguing. The connections can be too arbitrary. Yet these multiple-plotline novels are popular. If your idea is to write a book that is set in different eras, or concerns people in entirely different settings, I assume you have a very good idea that demands the parallel structure. I advise you to study novels you admire that use the structure you want to use. Describe the ways that lines of action and characters are connected and intersected; the ways that transitions are made; and, most of all, the themes that tie the plotlines together. You will need to think about all the issues I raise for each thread of the story *and* for the overall story. I realize that some very good writers use the multiple-story model successfully. Try to figure out why their books work. What you don't want to write is a book in which a reader gets bored with Plot B and skips ahead to see what's happening with the character she cares about in Plot A.

Now we can talk about how you organize plot, and how you organize the novel that develops it. Think of it as what you have in your head to guide you, and then how you put it on the pages.

ORGANIZING A STORY

The most common way to organize a story is chronologically. You start the story and continue until you reach the end. I venture to say that's the default for most apprentice writers. Basically, we expect stories to be told like that, from start to finish. The problem with this construct is that the story can be too loose. Find a way to frame the chronology. Give it an arrow to pull the reader through.

There are other ways to see a story. Perhaps your story takes place on two continents, and that gives you a natural organizer. Or the story covers a season (*Summer of My German Soldier*), a lifetime (*The World According to Garp*), or years of adolescence (*The Catcher in the Rye*). It could be an adventure—going out and making it back home, or not (*The Road*). Many stories are sagas (*Cold Mountain*) or epics (*American Pastoral*) that reflect the larger story of a time in history, or journeys that involve dramatic challenges (*The Bean Trees*), or an odyssey, like Colson Whitehead's *The Underground Railroad*.

A story could take place while a house is being built or a sick person is dying (*Benediction*; *Evening*). Organizers of time are probably the most common ways to get a handle on plot, but they certainly are not the only ones.

In *The Jane Austen Book Club*, Karen Joy Fowler used the once-a-month meetings of five women and the themes of Austen's novels to create a shape for the book. Amy Tan used the regular meetings of Chinese women to play mahjong as a way to tell their stories in *The Joy Luck Club*. Annie Proulx used maritime themes to emphasize the role of landscape in *The Shipping News*. *The Grapes of Wrath* is a journey. *The Stranger* is a man preparing to die. Many novels are basically fictional biographies (*Madame Bovary*; *Martin Eden*; *Angle of Repose*).

Many of my students want to start with a prologue. Sometimes I am able to help them instead develop a frame for the novel, opening it with a character who is old and looking back or young and looking forward. Truthfully, though, I discourage this approach because it is so hard to avoid clichés and confusion.

Once you start looking for organizers you will recognize them in everything you read. What you want to do is stand back from your own manuscript and "see it whole" as a shape or a theme, a reduction like the aboutness statement you worked on earlier. You are looking for a canopy, or perhaps a spine, something that feels complete as a unit.

It doesn't have to be complicated to be useful. When I wrote *Opal on Dry Ground*, about a mother who thinks it's her job to "save" her divorced daughters from their unhappiness, my organizer was very simple: The girls move in. The girls move out. The story is what happens in between, to nudge them along. In the first third of the book I was dealing with the women's unhappy stasis and the ways they kidded themselves about how they were living; then the novel shifted in the direction of its ending, as their lives began to open to new experiences and people and, inevitably, their independence.

In *Plain Seeing*, I covered a lot of years, but I saw them in blocks. The novel has two parts. The first is the story of Laura, the mother, from adolescence to her pregnancy with her daughter; the second is the story of her daughter, from *her* adolescence to her divorce and separation from *her* daughter. Just to liven that up a little (for me, as I was writing), I saw the mother's story as *either* what really happened to her, which her daughter can never know, *or* what the daughter invented because she had to have a story. *Walking Dunes* takes place over a school year and follows David's development into a young man, challenge by challenge, starting with a tennis game. *Beyond Deserving* is chronological, taking place over the summer of the Fisher boys' birthdays and their parents' fiftieth wedding anniversary.

To get this concept, just talk through novel after novel to yourself or with a friend. The light will come on. Look for the ways that chronology is handled; the themes that act as glue; the myths and cultural motifs that appear.

ORGANIZING A BOOK

The second organizer that I am talking about is how you *construct your book* as something that has a shape and parts.

Is it composed primarily of scenes, or does it have a lot of narrative summary in it? Many popular novels open each new chapter with a new scene that follows from the chapter before. The chapter is usually not a single scene, but a sequence of scenes. It leaves the story at a new place at the chapter end, and—voilà!—the next chapter picks it up with a new scene, perhaps opening with a bit of summary or commentary or description.

Others vary the chapter openings (my preference): sometimes a scene, sometimes some backstory, sometimes a description, or a summary that bridges time, and so on. Look over some novels and think of what you prefer, what draws you in to chapters. And think about what your idea of a chapter *is*.

One of your decisions is whether you want to end a chapter in a way that leaves the reader wondering what's coming next, or if you want to round off an event so that it is now part of the story history and you can move to something new. Probably you should vary endings. Obviously, how you end a chapter is important, because you establish an expectation and pattern in the reader's mind. Readers are more likely to set the book down at the end of a chapter (as opposed to stopping in the middle), and they can rightly expect either to wonder about the coming story or to feel satisfaction about something that just got settled. I can't see how anything can be right or wrong here, except that you want to establish a rhythm and expectation in the reader. For this same reason, I recommend your chapters be of similar lengths.

How many chapters should there be? I spent an hour in a

bookstore with this question in mind, and I was surprised to see that every book I looked at had from thirty to forty-five chapters. It didn't even seem to matter whether the book was long or short, because the chapters were relatively long and short as well. I don't think that constitutes a rule, but it gives you a start in thinking about your structure. Note, too, that authors sometimes break the novel into parts, calling them Part One, Part Two, etc., or Book One, Book Two. Sometimes the sections are titled: Eva's Book, Miranda's Book. Or they might be titled with dates, like Winter 1970. If the author uses multiple viewpoints, she might alternate them with chapter breaks, or use sections within the chapters. One thing I'd be careful about, though, is titling chapters or sections with dates, places, or people's names, without carefully considering how the text itself moves the reader to a new situation. Big shifts in context can be disorienting to the reader, and you want to create a transition that keeps the reader engaged and situated without having to glance back at the chapter title.

When I wrote my second novel I decided to be deliberate about how I would use chapters, and I considered my POV carefully. I ended up with some alternation of viewpoint, and I worked a long time to develop a timeline or "beat sheet" that gave me an outline of event steps through the story. Then I got a pack of five-by-seven-inch index cards, green and pink ones, and began dividing the story into chapters, one to a card. I gave Katie the green and Ursula the pink, so I could easily see the balance of my alternating POV. I worked on this for weeks, and I loved the ease with which I could switch things around, look back and forth, add notes, and lay out sequences. Once I had settled on chapters, I took each large card and a stack of smaller cards, wrote out scene summaries to capture the sequences within each chapter, and paper-clipped them together.

Once I was ready to rewrite, I worked from one card to the next. If, as I wrote, I realized I should have laid some groundwork earlier, I went back to a card and made a note in colored ink. Once I had a complete manuscript, I could fuss with the additional adjustments I had identified. After this experience I have used some version of the approach with every book, except with *Walking Dunes*, where I wrote long scenarios of sections before I began writing them. You'll see, in later exercises, the effect this has had on my view of the revision process. I have to say that I've never seen a way to approximate this process on the computer. The ease of the shuffle and the physical handling of the cards are integral to the process. I did add a wrinkle. Someone gave me some large sheets of cardstock paper and I liked laying my novel out on those, working from my cards to transpose major plot points. Then I could draw loops and lines and arrows and whatever else helped me see my connections and transitions in the plot. I could add questions and notes right on the large sheet, keeping the picture of the whole novel in front of me. I could put chapters across the top of the sheets, like headings, and list plot points beneath them, creating a visual map that I could take in with a single look. (It's important to remember, always, as you work with the bits and pieces of the manuscript, that you are constructing one thing: the novel.) Jane Smiley has written that she also makes charts to manage the many characters and events in her big novels. She uses intersecting columns.

I always tell writers to bring index cards to my workshops, and without any direction at all about how to use them, I notice that by the end of the second day they already have started stacks.

THERE'S ANOTHER, ENTIRELY different way to think about laying out and examining your novel's structure, and it is visual. Randy Ingermanson lays out a strategy he calls The Snowflake Method (http://www.advancedfictionwriting.com) that is a cohesive, practical design strategy. Likewise, I can imagine organizing a story as a tree with a trunk and several branches; a house of rooms; overlapping circles. Or you could give each viewpoint character a Lego color, and stack Lego bricks in a pleasing design, then see what happens when you transfer that to telling "Blue's" story and "Green's" story. You could have a colored Lego brick for each chapter, and stack them up to see your distribution. Braiding is a popular concept for planning, too; it's a variation on the alternating chapters idea, but it emphasizes the connections and interface of characters, and for that I think it is a useful idea. Timelines are a great place to start. For me, index cards have remained supreme: You can pick different colors for strands of the story; it's easy to move them around and test out organizational ideas; you can transfer summaries to large charts; and then you can make a neat little pile and get to work. Ultimately, of course, you have to move from the structure of your plan to the structure of your book.

Another approach to structure is to begin with three sentences and then expand them:

1. Opal's divorced daughters move in with her.
2. Opal tries to motivate them, but they stumble on their own new life turns.
3. Clancy has a baby; Joy moves to another state.

Those three statements encapsulate a novel, but also suggest the direction of events that it takes to develop the plot.

I've already talked a lot about writing sequences as links from event to event. You can see that if you start with a three-sentence summary, you can take each sentence and write such a sequence to get the characters from one step to the next.

1. Christopher sets out to solve the murder of a dog.
2. He discovers his mother is still alive and goes to look for her.
3. He ends up with two parents and two homes.

You may have done something like this in your original planning; now you can see if your initial idea provided a workable through line for the draft. Now is the time to amend it, or start from scratch and use the three-sentence summary to assess the sequence and proportions of your chapters.

BREAKS

How long is your novel? A big novel has to have a density that a shorter novel may not have. It has to engage the reader intellectually and emotionally enough to keep her reading, whereas a shorter novel may rely on plot progression to pull the reader along. Breaks are especially significant in long works. (If you want to see how a good writer manages a big plot with many characters, read a Richard Russo novel. He moves around in point of view, in a tumble of cross-purposes and alliances. His scenes are often riotous and always fully developed. You don't so much read as go along for the ride. I recommend an old novel, *Nobody's Fool* (1994), followed immediately by its sequel, *Everybody's Fool* (2016). (Maybe watch the movie of the first one in between!)

Breaks have two functions for the reader:

1. They give the reader a breathing place and, in some cases, a comfortable and logical place to put the book down.
2. They keep a hook in the reader so that she knows more is coming and that she will understand where she is in the story when she picks it up.

For you, the author, breaks function to identify arcs in the story line, depressions and accelerations in pace, and goalposts for reaching significant points in subplots.

You will probably want to look at your manuscript with

these ideas in mind, but I wouldn't worry about your breaks much yet. Chances are your manuscript will undergo a lot of changes and you will eventually want to think about your breaks—every single one.

A thought: Some genre fiction is remarkable for the density and length of its chapters. You'll know what I mean if that's your thing. What you want to do is study models to see how the writers organize and break chapters.

An important consideration is how you will organize blocks of text within chapters. Think about how you might use "white space" to indicate a passage of time, viewpoint, setting, or some other break in the narrative. (Don't decorate the space. That's a designer's job.) This is called a "section break" and it lets the reader take a breath, knowing he isn't going to lose the train of thought. *It is a significant break*, sort of a mini chapter break, so don't use it without considering why you want it at that particular point. For one thing, a reader may put the book down at that point; would that fit with your idea of the best way to read the book?

Every time you put in a break, consider why it belongs there. Don't use it because you ran out of steam. Don't use it when there is no real difference between what's on each side of the break. Don't use it every time you stop one scene and start another; that's what transition sentences and paragraph indentations are for. Apprentice writers overuse white space, as if they think it is a form of punctuation.

Remember that sections are units of the chapter, so you don't want a chapter and a section to have the same "weight" or significance in the overall narrative.

I wish I knew how to say something about short and long paragraphs, because I find that many of my students have no earthly idea why or when to break. They do so intuitively, which means they aren't giving consideration to the function of each paragraph. Working intuitively means sensing the rhythm of the flow of text, and many writers do have that gift; maybe it is a basic part of talent. But you probably know if your writing is boring or tangled syntactically at least part of the time. You can do something about it. I am not suggesting that a writer analyze every single paragraph, but it might be a good idea for an apprentice writer to take some time in a writing session to study a page and see what logic there is—or isn't—for the length and structure of paragraphs. (See Noah Lukeman's *A Dash of Style*, listed in "Recommended Books on Craft" in the Resources section.) And for heaven's sake, read your work aloud! Every paragraph. Every page. There's no better way to identify the clunky places.

Is this picky, time-consuming, and sometimes embarrassing? Yes. So it's better for you to do it consciously than for your reader to subconsciously reject your writing.

Don't let your manuscript run away from you. Stop now and then to survey its structure. You want the reader to sense organization and design, even if not consciously. You certainly don't want the reader to get lost.

EXERCISES

❑ Work with your stack of books. Reduce each to three sentences. Then consider how each "part" was developed in the novel. Take the time to write out the plot steps, and see how they are distributed over chapters.

❑ This is an exercise I would do first with a chapter from a model novel and then repeat using your manuscript.

Take a single chapter and describe its structure in detail. The first thing is to delineate the elements of narrative in the chapter. Here's a way to do it:

1. Find every scene and draw a rectangle around it. I call that a "scene block." If you discover that there's a whole lot in the passage *other than the scene action*, such as extended description or other exposition, put wiggly lines under those parts of the passage. Keep in mind that in

long scenes there may be compression, that is, passages of summary that are *essentially part of the scene.*

Later, come back to your scene and assess the function of the nonscenic elements of your scene block: the interiority, commentary, exposition. (Why is this here? What does it do for the story?)

2. With a different color, block out any extended narrative summaries or passages of exposition in the chapter that are not included in the scene blocks.

You'll do more extensive analyses later on, but for now this should tell you what the balance of scene and not-scene is in your chapter. There's not a right and wrong. You're just describing, at this point. Variety is nice. Now do it for another chapter, at least thirty pages away. It should interest you to see if your chapters follow a pattern of some kind in composition.

❑ Study the structures of as many novels as you can.

Start by describing the organizer for the novel.

Then flip through, look at the contents page, and see what the general layout is.

You can buy used books for a dollar these days. Mark them up, cut them up, learn from them. Tape model pages on the wall. Make a file. Find examples that help you design your own novel.

3. Write a tagline for each chapter—the list is a summary of your story.

It's a very simple exercise. Go chapter by chapter and say what happens. In a sentence or two. No details, just what it adds up to. If the chapter is a flashback or some other iteration of backstory, write a sentence of summary and put the notation **Hist** (history). If, however, there is present action, always put a sentence summarizing the action, even if there is also flashback in the chapter. (Chances are you'll have all kinds of mixes.)

Number your chapters.

If a chapter is *only* about a *subplot*, put **SP** (subplot) on that line. You want to be able to follow the major plot at a glance. If you want to do taglines for subplots—a good idea—do them on separate pages. Use a new line for each chapter if you are writing on paper, or use index cards, one for each chapter. The cards are handy because you can come back later to make lots of other notes. You could use white for main plot, and colors for subplots.

Some writers produce long chapters, some produce short, but a chapter should still lend itself to a summary. If long chapters have breaks and new plot points are introduced after the break, you'll need to put two separate one-sentence summaries for that chapter.

When you are done, you will have an outline of your novel. It's not a summary you'd send to an editor, but it ought to work for you.

Here I have written taglines for the first six chapters of Donna Leon's *The Waters of Eternal Youth*. Yes, it can be this simple, especially when, as in all of Leon's novels, the time frame of the story is short and everything proceeds chronologically. The story never goes to the past narratively, but it is revealed in the inspector's investigation in bits and pieces, until, at the end, it adds up. Think of the narrative of the crime hanging in space like fruit, and the author reaching up for ripe relevant details as she writes the present investigation.

I put two taglines if there is subplot in a chapter, so you can see how I differentiate plotlines. Doing the whole book, I would put the **SP** entries on separate pages.

1. At a fund-raising dinner, the wealthy patroness asks Inspector Brunetti to call on her privately.
2. Brunetti ponders the invitation with colleagues at work and calls to set up the meeting.
3. The contessa asks Brunetti to investigate an event from fifteen years ago, when her granddaughter was left brain damaged after being pulled from a canal. **Hist**

4. A continuation of the prior chapter, as the contessa explains more about her granddaughter's life. **Hist**

5. [SP At dinner that night, Brunetti's daughter Chiara tells about a young male immigrant who is routinely accosting her outside her school.]

6. [SP The next day, Brunetti asks his colleague Vianello to investigate the school problem], then **Plot** Brunetti starts to look into the history of the contessa's family and raises questions about some of the people who were at the fund-raising dinner.

As you can already see, a secondary plotline has been introduced—the matter of the immigrant harassment—and soon a couple other subplots begin (the girl's history at a riding school; the murder of the man who rescued the girl from the canal fifteen years ago). Everything is tightly woven but developed in a way that pulls in Brunetti's life at home, at work, with friends. (Leon's novels have a lot in common with so-called cozy mysteries.) The subplot with the immigrant is relatively independent; the other subplots converge in the revelations that accompany solving the old case.

Another writer who does something similar, except in France's Dordogne region, is Martin Walker, in his Bruno series. His novels are a little more complicated (they have more subplots) and livelier than Leon's, but they also have a policeman protagonist and a colorful setting. The Bruno books are more populated than the Italian ones, and Walker introduces themes about the intrusion of the outside world on his small community, from greedy truffle hunters to terrorists. There is also an arc of story over the course of the novel series, about local politics, Bruno's love life, and even his dogs.

Kent Haruf's novels, set in small-town Colorado, lend themselves to this exercise well, especially since he builds his stories mostly in scenes. On the other hand, you can go to a Jane Austen novel and find there is a great deal more exposition and commentary, but the progression of the plot is still easy to lay out in steps, chapter by chapter. And don't we love her commentary?

I urge you to do this exercise with a book you already know (you will be able to move quickly). It is instructive in a way that mere advice never can be.

Below are taglines for chapters that begin my novel *A Chance to See Egypt*. Chapters are titled but not numbered. I've chosen it because it doesn't follow a simple chronology and is quite intertwined with backstory. Chapters are, in turns, about widower Tom Riley's history with his wife and his honeymoon in Mexico; about his present experience in the same place; and also about other residents and their histories, including an American artist-turned-writer. There is more than one close point of view—more than one person (first and third), as well as an omniscient narrator who observes the village. Even in such a reduced form, I think you can see the story developing.

A Circus. Mr. Riley goes to a circus in a Mexican village.

At the Posada. Mr. Riley has settled into the hotel where he went with his wife on their honeymoon.

A Change of Direction. An artist narrator (Charlotte) tells how she left the New York art world and became a writer. **Hist, 1st POV**

A New Face. Tom Riley attends the writers' community workshop.

The Great House. Charlotte tells how she came to know Divina, a pretty local girl who becomes the artist's model. **Hist, 1st POV**

A Frequent Flyer. How Riley met his wife Eva and how he decided, after her death, to return to the place of their honeymoon. **Hist**

Simple Devotion. How Riley's dream of priesthood was lost and he was sent home to a different fate. **Hist**

A Christening. Riley follows the writing workshop by shuffling through his memories of Eva. **Hist**

An Independent Stroll. Riley sets out from the posada to see the village and meets up with Charlotte, who extends an offer of friendship and information about the village.

Good Intentions. Riley remembers meeting Father Bernal with his wife on their honeymoon. **Hist**

Eusebio. Eusebio and Divina climb an outcrop and talk about their dreams for the future; Divina's do not seem to include Eusebio.

A Slight Incline. Riley passes the day walking about, and meets a woman (Divina's mother) who runs a little food stand; she suggests he visit an interesting village nearby.

Dreamer. Divina models for the artist.

A Night in the Country. Riley visits Tapalpa and, missing his bus home, must take refuge in a local home.

Note that I am suggesting this exercise as part of an analysis of a model novel and/or a way of beginning the analysis of your own. Your outline will look different from mine, depending on your organization. You might not title your chapters, for example. What's important is that when you read through your taglines, you follow the spine of a story. Fuss with the descriptions. Eventually, you should have a version to guide your revision. It is a lot easier to make notes about structural changes on an outline like this than on pages of the manuscript. It is also easier to look across the sequence of events and assess the pace and the arc of action. If you are in a writing group, you will find you can discuss one another's stories constructively at the outline level.

I am definitely not saying this is a way to control a first draft; many writers, me included, work intuitively in the initial stages of a novel. But at some point you have to take stock of what you have, what you need, and what you are going to do about it.

If you study a novel that has structural qualities something like what you have in mind for your own, it is instructive to take the time to make a tagline list for at least the first quarter of the book, beyond the inciting event. You'll see how the writer "nests" the plot points in details and other activities, how they are relevant, and how the string of plot points is being laid out. *The more sophisticated the construction of the plot is, the more likely the chain of taglines will be broken by subplots and backstory.* (How does the author make transitions and connections?) Put your taglines on index cards, add notes about the scenes, and you have a storyboard of the novel. Use a different color for subplots.

Of course, when you reduce your own story to thirty or so sentences, you get a good idea of how strong the story line is.

A question: Are you finding a pattern in your use of the various structural components? For example, do you tend to have a scene, perhaps with some interiority, and then a passage of summary or description? Do you divide these up, perhaps with a white-space break? If this works for you, you may want to try for a fairly consistent pattern, plumping up some of the responses or descriptions where you have none.

Or do you use a lot of "telling"—long passages of exposition, commentary, and response? Plenty of writers do this very well, and so could you, but it's important to identify *where the action is*. You'll want to go through the manuscript marking all the parts where the plot is being moved along, where something is happening. You don't want those passages to be buried in exposition. This might mean the judicious use of white space, or some shifting about of the order in which passages are presented.

If all this talk of structural elements is making your eyes roll, but you know you have a story to tell, you might want to write a first novel in scenes. There would be description and perhaps some backstory, but the building block would be the scene. Many, many popular books are written like this. Mysteries. Children's and young adult books. Really, any book that "reads fast" is likely made up mostly of scenes.

EXERCISES

❑ Write taglines for a novel you have read recently—at least a substantial portion of it. It's also interesting to write them for a novel that felt very complex to you, especially if there was a lot of backstory. Then, of course, write them for your novel. *You can't do this exercise too many times. It is always instructive.* If you use different-colored Post-it Notes for the various threads (plot, subplots) and then lay them out on a board or wall in the relation they have in the book, you can see the construction of the book. It is an eye-opener. It is incredibly empowering. You'll stand there and think: I can do this.

❑ Write taglines for the steps of action in a chapter, whether they are scenes (in which case, title each one) or a combination of scene and summary. These are the beats of movement in the part of the story covered by the chapter.

❑ In a model novel, identify a subplot. What is the problem that has to be solved? (Or you could say, What is the question that has to be answered?) Write a summary of the subplot in three sentences. What is happening with the protagonist while this line of subplot is proceeding? What effect on the main plot does the subplot have?

❑ Now do the same exercise with a subplot in your novel. How does the subplot perk up the story line? Does it complicate it? How does solving the problem of the subplot relate to the main plot, or to the main character?

4. Evaluate your first chapter.

Before we can talk about how well the first chapter works, you have to consider a more basic and essential question: Did you start the novel in the right place? Take a few moments to look again at your narrative plotlines. Skim your chapter and notice where you have referred to past events. Put a squiggly line under every reference to the past. Could you leave those backstory references out, and use them in a later chapter? If they are essential, maybe the story wants to start earlier than you did. It is possible that you have chosen to write a kind of history as an opening salvo, but you'd have to be really good to get by with it. In general, we expect a novel to begin at the beginning; something happens in the first chapter that will lead into the rest of the book. If instead the chapter casts backward, you have to wonder if the second chapter is the first.

If you can find a novel that does just what you want to do—and it is wildly unconventional—believe me I think using the model as a jumping-off point is a great idea. If you love books with a voice that draws you into *someone* instead of to what's happening, maybe you can make that work for you. The key is going to be studying a lot of models and defining for yourself what the elements of your ideal opening are. Try several different openings. Come back later to think about it some more.

Look for a place to enter the story. All right, you already have, but I'm asking you to float your decision for a moment, because comparing it to other possibilities helps you evaluate it. Consider more than one way you could open the novel, weighing the dramatic effect of starting at that moment; the trajectory toward the climax; the need for exposition of what went before; etc. You want a story opening that is compressed enough to create tension (it raises a question) but elaborated enough to introduce aspects of character, plot, and theme. Try writing *two new sentences to begin the first chapter*. You may discover something you can use to improve what you have already done. Read into your chapter and see if you can find a new opening lying in wait.

You probably have already heard or read advice about jumping right into the action, creating suspense, and raising a big question about what will follow. Some books require a heavy-action start, but I have a different expectation of first chapters. If you can introduce the story question that early, fine; perhaps you can introduce a deeper question, the something in the protagonist that hurts or makes a demand. But what you *must* do is establish the sound of your voice.

I think the primary function of the first chapter is to establish the writer's contract with the reader:

> *Here is the narrator, and this is the voice you will hear.*
> *Here is a person you will come to know and care about.*
> *This is the pace of things, the way I lay prose on the page.*
> *This is how big a chapter is and how fast it reads.*
> *This is a story that will make you laugh; draw you into compassion and sorrow; pull you along with suspense; fill your pockets with information and commentary; take you to exotic places; explore the drama of a small world; and so on!*

WHAT WILL YOUR NOVEL DO?

The reader should know what she is getting into. Personally, I don't consider tension in the first chapter all that important; often it feels artificial, and I dislike the feeling I'm being manipulated. Someone can tell me that Novel X is the best read ever, but if I don't fall in love with the sound of the narration, the intelligence of the sentences, the feeling of being drawn into the consciousness of someone intriguing and deep and mysterious, I'm just not interested. If I try to write like that myself, and it puts off the reader who is looking for a romp and a fast ride, that is fine with me. If you are writing an adventure story, a suspense novel, or a thriller, you will surely know what you have to do in the first chapter, because you will have read a lot of other novels like what you are writing. You want your first chapter to give the reader a good idea of what the novel is going to be like.

So how the chapter sounds lets the reader know what kind

of consciousness is guiding the story. *Then* you can worry about what question(s) you raise. Not, already, "Will Samantha escape the burning house?" but "Who is Samantha? What is she looking for and where will her search take her?"

Here we are, the first chapter says. *Come in.*

Sometimes, an event occurs in the first chapter that sets things moving; this isn't necessarily the "catalytic" or "inciting" event that raises the big story questions. Rather, the opening event creates context. Bernard Grebanier calls this "establishing the ground for the story." Turning the soil. Opening some doors. Lighting a lamp. The first thing that has to happen in order for the next thing—the more dramatic thing—to happen.

A child is born but given away and the mother is told the child died.

Two boys set out to ride across the border into adventure.

A shamed woman flees to a resort to give things time to calm down.

A dog is killed and a boy decides to find out who did it.

A mother on an errand in World War II–era San Francisco sees the notice requiring all people of Japanese ethnicity to report to transfer centers.

A small boat carrying a very pretty woman approaches a totally out-of-the-way Greek village.

A woman is asked by her government's secret service to take on one more assignment.

Note that the catalyst doesn't have to be big and brassy. In the first chapter of Sue Miller's *The Good Mother,* the scenes seem to function merely as information, a look at the relationship of mother and child, which we know will somehow be sundered. But consider what happens after the mother picks up a letter at the post office. She carries it all through the day and evening, until she finally reads it. It's a minor matter related to her impending divorce. You hardly notice it, but the repeated appearance of the letter creates a subliminal expectation in a reader: Something more is ahead. It's like the trickle into a thread of water into a stream into a river. The divorce makes her vulnerable, though she expresses confidence that it's being handled very amicably and efficiently. The letter is significant in the same way the first cut in fabric is significant; the way the car turns when it backs out of the driveway. It doesn't have to feel portentous at the time, it just has to be the first step.

There are a few good general rules in writing a first chapter, such as:

Don't get bogged down in describing the setting. Unless, of course, the novel is about an adventure on the great cold Atlantic and so that's the first thing you want the reader to know. Unless it's a tale of the Civil War and you open on a battlefield littered with corpses. Unless it's about a murder on a movie set. You get the idea.

Don't try to set up what's coming by telling what happened before. I'm sure you'll find an exception. But it's still basic advice: Start the novel where the story starts. Don't launch into a setup. The reader wants to *be there*, not hear history. As long as you keep in mind that you are beginning the story, you'll do the right thing.

Don't try to "hook" the reader by jumping ahead to something really, really exciting and mysterious. Also known as a prologue. There are certain genres where prologues are acceptable, but I think they are a bad idea. If you can't get your reader's attention in the *right now* of the story, find a different place to begin telling it. Sometimes, instead of a prologue—a piece of story to come later—an author begins his novel with a meditation on an aspect of life, family, fate. It's a risky and challenging approach, requiring a strong voice, the ability to carry the reader into abstractions, etc., but it can be very satisfying and attractive, too. Such an opening should segue into something active, in that first chapter.

Don't get lost in explaining why what is happening matters, or what the character is thinking about. I know I'm repeating myself; it bears repeating. Let the unwinding of event pull the reader into the story.

The single best thing you can do now is to look at many sample beginnings: first lines; first paragraphs; first pages; first scenes; first chapters. Take a stack of books to the bookstore coffee shop. Get your cappuccino and read openings. Take notes that describe what you observe that you like. Try out strategies with your own story, like doing calisthenics. Take a break and then sum up what you most liked and what seemed most helpful to you in writing or evaluating your own opening.

In the first chapter of *The Curious Incident of the Dog in the Night-Time* the boy Christopher discovers the neighbor's dog, still warm, but dead. It actually takes five short chapters to introduce the story problem—he is accused wrongly of killing the dog and then undertakes to solve the murder. First he tells the reader who he is and what he is like. Each brief chapter is charming and intriguing. The voice is definitely the come-hither element.

Madame Bovary, interestingly, does not begin with Emma. It delays introducing her, making the reader wait—and a reader does want to get a first glimpse of her. But the early chapters create the world in which Emma and Charles will meet and marry. It is all about time and place and chance. It is *interesting*. It is also a novel from the nineteenth century, when books didn't have to compete with television and movies.

The first chapter of *The Last Painting of Sara de Vos* is a different case. It is all a scene in the elegant Manhattan apartment of the protagonist and his wife, a $500-a-plate charity dinner. Other rich people are mingling about. Some odd people show up (they were hired to come) and make a scene. I liked it well enough to keep reading, but I think it was the weakest part of the novel. It was a setup for the theft of the painting hanging in the bedroom, but characters were introduced that we never saw again, the threat that an intruder would ruin the party didn't lead to anything, and I was relieved when it was over. Mind you, it meant more *later*, but it would not have made me buy the book if I hadn't read a review and been intrigued by the subject (art forgery) ahead of time.

EXERCISES

❏ Read the first chapter of a novel you love. Describe the voice. What expectations are raised for what is coming? How would you describe the contract the author offers you as reader?

Repeat with many novels!

❏ Now work your way through this evaluation list with your own novel.

1. Does this chapter truly begin the story? (In other words, will the next chapter pick up where it left off? If not, what is the chapter tied to eventually?) Is it *not* making any false promises?

2. Is this chapter written in the voice of the novel from now on? Is there irony? compassion? sorrow? delight? gravity? buoyancy? Decide what effect you think you have established *and point to the specific sentences that build it.*

3. Do you think the reader will feel drawn in and swept along by the sense of having entered a large story to come?

4. Is there a sense of a *story question* being raised? This can be one or both of two kinds of questions: (a) an immediate problem or (b) an overarching problem. You get a gold star if you do both. You get it later if your opening chapter is about context and is so interesting we don't care that we have to wait for the problem.

5. Is the first sentence perfect? Read it aloud. Several times. Read the first sentence of lots of novels. There's also a feature in each issue of *Poets & Writers* that presents first sentences.

6. Do you think the reader will rightly expect the story to be laid out the way it is, in terms of chapter lengths, for example?

7. *Write out* what your chapter establishes about the story as a whole. This isn't saying what happens in the chapter, it's saying what expectations are being raised, what the reader will assume about the experience of reading your book. (Of course she won't know what's going to happen.)

8. Does your chapter have a beginning, middle, and end? What is its balance of narrative summary and scene? Does that represent your style throughout the book? Is there satisfaction in reading the chapter, as if it is a story of its own?

9. Does your first chapter make your heart thump? (And I do mean yours, not the reader's, necessarily. I mean: Right now, reading it, are you excited about your book?)

5. Choose six noncontiguous scenes and describe how they connect across the plot.

How do scenes connect? Well, one leads to the other. But I am asking you to read six *disconnected* scenes. The logic of the ongoing action won't lull you from your evaluation. Each scene has to be successful; all scenes have to have something viable to do with the overall story.

This is a little tricky. I want you to choose any six scenes you like, from six different chapters. Pull those chapters from your hard copy and lay them out in consecutive order. The scenes won't—indeed, should not—follow one right after the other, one, two, etc. This is random sampling, but I wouldn't use all scenes that you know are among the most important ones; you'll get to them later. They don't have to be long scenes, but they need to be long enough to have action, tension, a turning point, character response (all of the things a good scene has).

Of course every scene should contribute to the forward movement of your story. Otherwise, what is it doing there? If this turns out to be a way to catch a weak scene, all the better. You can tag it for rewrite right now.

So your six scenes might look like this:

From chapter 3, second scene.
From chapter 7, first scene.
From chapter 13, third scene.
From chapter 15, third scene.
From chapter 24, first scene.
From chapter 33, last scene.

Start by writing a brief summary of each scene, just a few lines. Write it at the top, or on a sticky note.

Identify the "high point" or turning point of each scene and mark it in some way. Consider how it moves the plot forward. Or does it serve some other function, such as deepening understanding of the protagonist? Is it part of the "now" of the novel, or is it part of the backstory? Describe its function on a sticky note. Seeing a scene out of context is an arbitrary thing to do, but it helps you cast a cold eye on it.

Read the scenes one by one as separate entities. Is the scene interesting, never mind that it might refer to things that came before? Remember that you have no ticket to skip pages, or paragraphs, or sentences. Everything must interest the reader. Choose a page at random and note the details: the scum on the dishwater, the faint sound of giggling through the walls, light striking the rim of a glass. Everything alive, evocative, belonging, *interesting*.

Does the passage have heft? *Does it need to be a scene?* Does it feel like a little story, with a beginning, a middle, and an end? Or is it a scene introduced as a placeholder for a passage of backstory or response? *What is its function?*

If I were a reader, and I opened the book to this scene as a sample of the book, would it make me want to read the rest of it?

If you don't like the answers to these questions about a particular scene, you know you need to consider whether it belongs in the novel at all, and if it does, you need to rewrite it.

Now skim the scenes and study your notes. How do the scenes connect? If it's not evident that they connect plot points, consider the settings, the tone, the characters. Do they sound as if they are from the same book? Are there any echoes from one of the scenes to another? If the protagonist is in all of them, is he a consistent character, without being repetitive? Has something happened to him between the first and the sixth scene that affects his behavior? If he isn't in a scene, can you connect the character who is there to the other scenes? Do you feel there is a stream going by and these are six times you have stepped into it?

Write out your answer. I would start by saying how one scene connects to the next one—in the example above, chapter 3 to chapter 7. (If nothing else, time will have passed. Does anything that happened in chapter 3 seem to affect what happened in chapter 7?) Does the later scene have any "seed" in the first scene that has been developed by this scene? Are there different characters in the scenes? Does the second scene push any plot point raised in the first scene? How has the character changed from an early scene to a later one?

Then go to the next pair—chapter 7 and chapter 13—and so on; in each dyad, consider how one scene has jumped in time and plot progression to the second one. In essence, you are considering the elisions—what has come between them.

Can you tell that the story has been driven by complications that intensify?

If you have chosen scenes that are not closely connected, there will be some sense of disjunction in the set. However, they should read as excerpts from the same story; they should have connective tissue, even if it is subtle. They should indicate rising (and perhaps falling) action—that is, complication. What happens in, say, the fourth scene should depend in some way on what happened in the earlier scenes. You are putting a dipstick into your manuscript; you want to see if the same fluid is running under all its pages.

What do you think of the way these scenes relate—to one another, to the story as a whole? As samples, would they make a reader want to read more? What kinds of questions do the scenes raise? How important are those questions to the novel? Is there tension?

If one of your scenes is wimpy, do something now: Decide why you wrote it, what it was supposed to accomplish. Then find a way to fold that into another scene and eliminate this one. If you thought this was an important scene, it has to be dramatic. It has to have energy and conflict. What complication can you add or intensify?

If you think the scenes are too disparate, make notes about the elements that seem "off." See if there are ways to make these separated scenes more like relatives instead of strangers.

EXERCISES

❏ Consider doing this first with the novel you have chosen to study.

For each scene, find a moment you can capture in a "snapshot." Freeze time. You take a photograph of that moment in your mind. Write a caption for it on a piece of paper. Now lay the papers out and think about the snapshots laid out side by side. Envision the snapshots—those moments caught in time. Are they intriguing? Do they seem to belong together? Is there a sense of mystery in them? Do you wonder what the connections are? Why did you choose each one?

For each scene, identify the highest point of tension. How is it related to the overall question of the plot?

Where is this photograph taken (the setting at this point in the story)? Is there something special about *this moment, in this place*?

❏ Take any two of the scenes and answer these questions:

1. What is there in both scenes that makes them recognizable as being from the same story?

2. What is there in each scene that makes it different from any of the other scenes?

3. How is the world of the novel brought to life in each scene?

4. What has changed for the character(s) from an earlier scene to a later one? Can you heighten that change? Identify the emotion of each scene and make it stronger? How can we tell whose scene it is? How does it relate to what that character wants? In the second scene, is the character closer to what he wants, or does it seem even further away? What does this do to how he feels? Can you make his greatest need energize this scene?

Does this scene heighten your character's strengths or flaws? (Either is good, if it is the right time, if it affects the road to the character's transformation.)

❏ Now take two scenes that have at least two scenes in between. Read your captions of the four scenes. Is there any way that you could get from the first scene to the fourth *without the interim scenes—or without one of them*? In other words, is there enough tension to justify all of these scenes, or can elements be collapsed?

❏ List the settings for each of the six scenes. If some are the same, is that by default, or is it because it is exactly the right setting? Is there something about the settings that, taken as a group, help to develop the world of the novel?

Consider whether any of your scenes could be eliminated as stand-alone scenes, and instead collapsed into what comes before or after the scene.

❑ Which scene presents your protagonist with the biggest threat of loss? If you have chosen six scenes and none of them have the dramatic energy of conflict and complication, you know this is something you will have to work for throughout the manuscript when you do scene sequences.

For now, choose any of the six scenes and rewrite it. Make things worse for the character. Add a passage of deep interiority when the character has to admit failure, face a threat, or simply wonder how to go on from this place.

6. Mark the scenes to indicate backstory. Evaluate for relevance, economy, trigger, and transition.

Now go through each of your six scenes and, with a pen or marker, block out any backstory that arose in the scene. Describe the backstory in terms you have been introduced to so far.

Does the reference to the past matter *right now*?

What brings up the memory of the past?

Is the backstory presented as narrative summary; is there a flashback passage; or does someone bring the memory up in dialogue? If the memory isn't talked about, is someone thinking about it, or is it "stuck in" by the narration?

How does the passage return to present time and action, leaving the backstory behind?

Did you feel the backstory interrupts the scene or contributes to it?

The purpose of reviewing the use of backstory is simply to think about it one more time. It may be fine. But if you are uneasy, consider whether it really belongs in the text in this place, if ever.

You wouldn't expect backstory to appear in the same way in all or even most of the six scenes. Could you make your introductions of the past more varied? At the same time, are you obviously "dipping" into the same well of experience, and if so, is that deliberate? Effective?

Is the same thing coming up over and over? If so, how is it deepening and taking on more meaning with each new reference?

7. Mark passages of summary and exposition, and evaluate.

This may overlap with marking backstory in the previous step. In this case you are going to mark all the text that is not the action of the scene, including:

1. Any summary of action, which might be present ongoing and therefore a part of the scene, compressed.
2. Any summary of past action.
3. Any presentation of information that adds to what could be known by reading only the action of the scene.
4. Any history and description, which might also include commentary by the voice of the narration.

The same questions apply: Do you need it? Do you need it now? Is it comfortably nested or do you need to adjust transitions?

If you are sure you need the exposition, take the time to articulate why that would be. Is it explaining something *happening in the scene* that would be confusing otherwise? Is it referring to something in the past that makes the scene action easier to understand?

How do you help the reader make the transition from

summary or exposition back into the scene? Point to the specific sentence or phrase that accomplishes this.

8. Mark passages of interiority, and evaluate.

Here you mark those passages wherein a character is *thinking*, in contrast to where the character is speaking or acting.

Is she thinking about something in the past?
Is she thinking about what is happening now?
Is she wondering what is coming next?
Furthermore, do the character's thoughts affect what she
    does next?

Read through the scene again.

Do you think that the interiority interrupts or slows down the scene? Does it contribute to tension (perhaps through the contrast of character thought and action) or meaning (as the character interprets the scene)? Is it interesting? (Here's the hard question: Would a reader skim right over it?)

Does the interiority take us into the emotions and intellect of the character so that we understand better the meaning of this scene and of other elements of the story? In other words, do we learn more about the character, and empathize with her deeply?

How does the interiority affect the pace of the chapter? It probably slows it down. Is this a good thing? (Is this a good place to pause from the ongoing narrative and enter the consciousness of the character, feel with her, worry with her, etc.?)

Does the interiority have within it some kind of conflict and tension? For example, is the character trying to make a decision with large consequences? Or is she reconsidering past events and seeing them in a new way, therefore changing what she will do now?

You should be able to describe exactly what is going on in the thinking. If your character is torn between two needs or desires, between choices, between decisions, the interiority has a lot more impact than just thinking in general. This is especially true if both choices seem wrong but a decision has to be made.

In the end the question is: Do you need the interiority? Does it add to the quality of the scene?

Could any of the six scenes be trimmed?

Should any of them have additional interiority?

Is there a consistent theme running through the interiority, across the six scenes?

EXERCISES

❑ Write out a scene like a play. Write down only dialogue and actions (stage directions). Compare that to your scene; as you add back each bit of interiority, judge its worthiness of inclusion.

Now read through all the lines of interiority. Using them as a launch, write a passage that could appear at the end of the scene, with none of the interiority appearing within the scene. How do the two strategies compare? Did you discover anything new in the extended passage?

❑ Go through ten consecutive pages of your manuscript—you can select them randomly or for any reason you want—and double-underline all interiority.

Now label in the margin the kind of interiority each instance is.

Is it response, reflection, interrogation, or exposition?

Is it concerned with the past, the present, or the future?

Consider whether you have a set pattern, using mostly one kind of interiority, or if you vary your choices.

Consider if you have exploited any opportunities to draw on backstory in passages of interiority.

I RECENTLY HAD a workshop group do this with their novel manuscripts for most of an hour. They were cooperative but not enthusiastic; they didn't really see the point. At the end, though, when they evaluated their survey, they were surprised by how limited their use of various kinds of interior thinking was, and each expressed resolution to go through her entire novel to see if she could more effectively build and reveal character through more considered interiority.

9. Choose two key scenes and evaluate them using a scene template.

You can do this with any scenes you want. I suggest that you choose one that you have good feelings about and another that you have a sneaky suspicion might need reinforcement.

If you identify a weakness or a question about the scene, tag it or write a note on the blank manuscript page opposite it, so that you can come back to it later.

Give your scene a caption that captures the essence of its event, then analyze it.

Scene template

1. Do I have a clear purpose for this scene, and does the scene satisfy it? (Think of functions like: confrontation, decision, catalyst, turning point, capitulation.)
2. Is it dramatic? (This would mean conflict, rising action.)
3. Are there passages of flashback, description, or interior response? Do they break up the flow of the scene? If so, can they be reduced or eliminated? Alternatively, do I need more emotional ballast in the scene, and does this mean I should add interiority? Would this be a good

place to slow down the story and enter the consciousness of the character deeply?

4. Are the beats of action clear? Do they build to a high point of drama?

5. Have I "grounded" the scene in its setting? Does the scene convey a sense of being somewhere? How are the senses used: things seen, smelled, heard?

6. Is the viewpoint clear? Is there a clear goal or intention for the viewpoint character?

When you have analyzed sample scenes, you will have a good feeling for how you have handled scenes and also how the novel "holds together." Remember that although a novel is long, there is no room for slack. Every page matters.

See "Scene Template" in the Resources section for further analysis questions.

Pause

Look through the notes you have made so far. Do a little organizing.

Take a break.

Come back. Use your observations to evaluate your draft globally.

In general:

Does it fulfill your vision for the novel (even roughly)? Does the structure hold and support your story? Does the point of view work?

Identify stumbling blocks. Write notes on the manuscript.

Write your reflections on what you have learned about your draft so far, and what issues must be addressed in revision.

Consider reviewing scene-writing skills in preparation for revision.

Rework some of the exercises. Study your model novels.

Two: The Plan

I HAVE A lot less to say in this section, except where I introduce a new concept like "lines of threads." By now you should have a lot of notes and questions from the chapters you have read and the description you have written. Look back to earlier in this book to review ideas and exercises suggested there. Review your statement of aboutness.

My goal here is to help you organize a plan for revising your novel. Thus, the concepts are extensions of what you have studied in the earlier sections.

How do I revise?

1. Write a capsule summary of the plot, emphasizing the story problem, the crisis point, and the resolution.
2. Write a new summary of the novel.
3. Write a brief summary of your protagonist's fate and explain how it fulfills your vision for the novel.
4. Develop a scheme of core scenes.

5. Develop a scheme of lines of threads.
6. Identify key scene sequences in each plot movement.
7. Identify passages, scenes, and chapters from the first draft that will be used in the revision.
8. Identify passages, scenes, and chapters that need new drafts.
9. Decide whether you will amend your first draft or begin again with a new manuscript.
10. Write a document that describes your love of your story.

Summaries

1. Write a capsule summary of the plot, emphasizing the story problem, the crisis point, and the resolution.

You have chosen to write a novel that is *predominantly* a novel of story (character) *or* a novel of plot. Either way, both action and meaning are developed, but right now, consider which approach you are more committed to. Then, if you like, write the other summary as well. Keep these points in mind, though:

1. A novel of story (character) is going to be about the protagonist's journey in the context of the plot—but the character is the real subject. Depth, complexity, inner conflict, empathy— these are the qualities of the character that are developed by the plot. A paragraph summary is adequate.

2. A novel of plot has a strong story line with twists and turns, questions and suspense, crisis and high tension, and a resolution that pulls everything together. Consider your protagonist's journey as one of overcoming obstacles and arriving at a solution or achievement; of vanquishing an antagonist or

circumstances that were a threat to the well-being of the protagonist and those he cared for. Three short paragraphs would follow the prescription.

2. Write a new summary of the novel.

Do not feel tied to your draft!

Develop the summary in three "movements" (three long paragraphs):

1. Opening and establishing story ground and questions.
2. Developing and complicating plot.
3. Intensifying and resolving plot.

You will be using your summary from now on in other exercises. You are creating a blueprint for revision.

Don't skip this step. Don't rush. This is deeper and more expansive than your warm-up exercise above.

A reminder: Writing in summary frees you from the pressure of finding the "right" words, of shaping the scenes—all of the self-consciousness of getting things on the page. You are thinking about story, not style. This is for you, not a reader.

You might start by telling the story in three sentences. I'm not sure why, but my students love this exercise. I think it clarifies story, for one thing; and it testifies that there actually *is* a story. Some of my students have then taken each sentence, one by one, and "peeled" it by expanding it into three new sentences. So now you have a summary of nine sentences. Then you can start making sequences between sentences. It's sort of like greasing your skis; it gets you going.

Sit down away from your manuscript and your notes, preferably after a few days of rest from the work. Then tell your story. Don't worry about sticking to the draft. Don't spend much time brooding over the ideas for changes that come up. Don't worry about whether it's long or short. Don't worry about the "parts" right now. Just sit down and tell the story in a summary form. Imagine yourself speaking: *Here is a story.*

Let yourself be caught up in the flow of narrative, and if something occurs that surprises you, don't stop to consider whether it really belongs.

After you have written such a free-flowing draft, you can study it, scratch your head, and consider whether to write it over again. You can think about what ideas for changes popped up. You can identify still-not-quite-decided points. You might want to look back over all the notes you have taken up to this point. Perhaps amend this new summary based on your compiled observations. *What you want now is a guide to take you into revision.* It can have some questions and some "maybes" in it. Your summary should capture enough that you feel that the story is coherent, dramatic, and structured. The summary is about *what happens.* It doesn't include backstory, commentary, interiority. If you feel that the novel is very much about those latter things, I suggest that you write a page that summarizes the backstory and describes how it impinges on the story; write a separate page that talks about the meaning. Get it out of your system. Give yourself some distance by writing it out. Think it through away from the manuscript.

You could do this in three to five pages. Or you could write fifteen to twenty pages. It depends on the length and complexity of the story and on your impulse. I like to do both—a short version, then a longer one. If your story has parallel plots of more or less equal weight, I would treat them in two separate plot summaries. There will be overlap. Or you can write the summary in sections, alternating the same way that it appears in your draft. If it helps you, write summaries of the subplots, but we will be looking at those shortly.

You should be able to look over your summary and identify places where the story clearly should be told in scenes. Other parts may be told in summary. Don't automatically use the scheme of scenes you have already written; stay open to fresh ideas. Indicate these sections with colored pens, stars, check-marks, or whatever works for you. Think: *scene* and *summary*. Underline a few lines that indicate *big scenes*. Why are they big ("obligatory") scenes? What turns in them? What follows them? *Is a clock ticking in any of them*, i.e., is there something that must happen before it is too late?

You may want to write the summary more than once. It's not an exam, there aren't time limits. You want to feel satisfied that you have captured the story. As you continue through the revision process, continue to make adjustments. If writing the summary gives you ideas for scenes in your draft, go back to the bound copy and make notes.

Trust the process.

THE SECOND PART of this exercise will help you pin the story down more specifically. *You are going to rewrite your summary in three sections.*

Start a new page for each section.

1. *Beginning.* Start at the beginning and tell what happens far enough into the story that you have established *who* and *where* and *what* and *how* there is a *story question* that will pull the reader into the next movement of the novel. Think about the *ground for the story*, the circumstances that have come to-gether to create a situation that creates a problem. Identify the *catalyst*, the event that launches the plot. What happens that pushes the protagonist into a chute she can't get out of? (She may not know it yet.) This summary will probably cover several chapters, around a quarter of the book.

State the story problem. Write a passage that tells what the protagonist feels about it, what she is scared of, what she wants, who she hopes will help her. Spell out *where she is at this moment*. This isn't for the manuscript, it's for you, so let it roll without any worry about how it sounds.

2. *Middle.* Spell out the steps of *complication* that increase the tension, deepen the reader's concern for the protagonist and other characters, and take her to the point where cymbals crash. (This can be quieter than it sounds, especially in a literary novel, but what isn't "big" is "deep." Literary characters have to have obstacles that thwart them, too, even if they turn out to be internal.) Identify the scene where things seem impossible to solve, where the character is facing loss or defeat or failure. You should be able to write a list of captions or sentences that spell out the beats (steps) in the complicating of the story problem. Think of yourself laying out a map of the story, with hills and valleys. Avoid crowding the story with excessive or tangential complications.

3. *End.* Describe the highest point of *tension*, the aftermath, and "how things work out." Has the protagonist achieved her goals? Has someone won and someone lost? Is there harmony? What is the emotional tenor of the ending? (Should the reader feel sad, mad, glad, etc.?) Were there surprises in this line of events? Again, write freely about how the protagonist feels in that point of great conflict, and how she feels when the problem is solved (satisfactorily or not).

Go back to your opening chapters and revisit the question raised there. Can you point to places that establish the ground for the story? The place where the plot is set in motion? Where the story question is established? Do you feel now that the novel does in fact answer that question? That the action began there and moved inevitably (but not obviously) toward the conclusion?

4. *Interiority and commentary.* Now go through your summaries and indicate places where you know you are writing about backstory, or you have *extended* description or interiority. For example:

Here is where I finally reveal how Jeremy died.
Here is where, through a long night of contemplation,
    Elise makes the decision to divorce Ben.

Here I describe how the house and property have been left after the ravages of the fire.

This is where I explain John's role in the failure of the company.

Here the narrator talks about all the ways the doctors missed Patricia's diagnosis.

A mother can't see evil in her son.

Remember that you are no longer bound to your first draft. Make changes to improve the story. Try different schemes. Take your time.

Now you can pull together possibilities for your revision: holes in the story; imbalances in scenes; limpness of character; over- or underwriting of interiority; use of backstory.

Give yourself some time to pull out the stops. Look at a turning point and imagine how you could punch it up, make it more dramatic, make it matter more. Where there's blood, add guts. Where there's tears, add screams. I exaggerate, of course, but *considering* ways to build more drama can't hurt.

TURN THIS SUMMARY exercise into something visual. Write a caption for each of the three movements of the plot, across the top of a sheet of paper. Down the left side list your chapter numbers. Now go down the chapters and put a checkmark in the movement where it belongs. Look at the balance of chapters. You should have most of your chapters in the middle section. If you don't, think about the beginning and ending sections again, and whether there are chapters that should be tied more closely to that middle movement.

At the "hinge" between movements (going from a to b and b to c) you should be able to identify the scene where there is a *shift in plot and tension and mood*. Those should be places where a reader might set the book down with a sense of anticipation and concern (a to b) and then heightened concern and anticipation (b to c). In each case, there should be a sense that *the story has moved forward to a new place.*

If you make a large chart like this and leave room for sticky notes, you can make additions and other changes as you progress.

STORY PROBLEMS

Now think of your novel in terms of story problem. This is one more way to set you up for what is forward motion in the novel; for raising questions that have to be answered and that, in answering, require the protagonist to act.

Here are some sample story problems, with just a few questions that immediately bubble up.

The Curious Incident of the Dog in the Night-Time

Christopher wants to find out who killed the neighbor's dog. And when he learns in the investigation that his absent mother is alive, he wants to find her. (He's never left town alone. Can he manage the trip? Will his mother want him?)

The Last Painting of Sara de Vos

Martin wants to punish the woman who forged his seventeenth-century painting. Forty years later, he wants to atone for the way he did so. (Is it possible? Will she care? And besides, she lives on another continent now!)

More Than Allies

Two mothers want to find a way to reunite their sons with the boys' fathers. (Can they forgive the men their trespasses? Can they leave the only homes they know?)

The Good Mother

Anna has to fight for custody of her daughter—and cope with her self-blame. (Now that she's been wrongly, badly punished for her sexuality, will she forever reject her lover?)

The Piano Maker

Helene wants a quiet good life with work and small comforts. But she is arrested for a crime she was already absolved of. (Can she once again, and finally, defend her innocence?)

The Great Gatsby

Jay Gatsby has spent years building a fortune so that he can win back the love of Daisy, who is married to a bullying, immensely wealthy man. (Will Daisy want him? What will the husband do? *Who are these people?*)

The Indian Bride

The police want to find out what happened to a woman who got off a plane in Norway and disappeared; assuming she has been murdered, they want to find the murderer. (First, if there's a body, where is it? What villager would murder a woman he doesn't even know?)

All the Pretty Horses

John Grady wants to marry the rancher's daughter, but he must save his own life. (How does he escape the father, and after that, prison? How does he survive the terrible journey home?)

Benediction

A man with terminal cancer wants to die a good death. (What wrongs have to be righted? Who isn't there to say good-bye?)

The Member of the Wedding

Frankie feels she doesn't belong to anyone, anywhere. (Where does she want to fit in? Who will recognize her personhood?)

A House for Mr. Biswas

Biswas wants to own his own home and be his own boss, instead of being controlled by his wife's family. (What will he do, and do, and do, trying to be independent? How will he bear the humiliations of his failures?)

The Stranger

In a moment of blind, pointless rage, a man shoots another man to death on a sand dune and is sentenced to death. (How will he ever understand what he did, and how can he accept his fate, which is so cruel and final?)

For any story problem, you can immediately see that there are associated questions and needs; that reaching one step in a search can mean having to climb another.

What makes a good story problem?

It has no easy answer.

It matters a lot.

It challenges the protagonist in emotional and moral ways. In a plot-driven novel, there may be physical challenges.

What makes a bad story problem?
Who cares? It's too familiar, too shallow.
It can be solved too quickly.
It's overcomplicated.

UNUSUAL PLOT DESIGNS

Are you thinking that your unusual structure doesn't fit this scheme for analysis? I can't cover all the possibilities for structural innovation, but I will say this: Chronology is your best friend. No matter the order in which you tell the story, you must have a sound story to tell. If you know your story in the most basic logical order, you won't get lost when you distort it for effect. Start with an analysis that is chronological, from the impetus for the story, through the twists and turns, to the resolution. When you are satisfied that your plot sits well on this straight line, you can more confidently look at how you are mixing time frames, points of view, settings, or whatever you are using in your innovation. You'll know all the building blocks as you make your special design.

However you present your story—the design of its telling—you have the same general concerns as the most conventional writer. You want to draw the reader in, pose questions that engage, and then build the escalation of concern and event that is a story. You may want to puzzle the reader, but you never want to frustrate her. Anytime you "pull a switcheroo" in a timeline, be sure you think about what you've left, what you are entering, and what expectations you are setting. There have to be points of satisfaction even along the trail of a mystery.

MORE ABOUT SUBPLOTS

If your subplots involve a lot of action that doesn't include the protagonist, I suggest that you lay out the steps of scenes for them just as you do for the plot. A subplot is, after all, a story.

It has an arc; things happen; it reflects your vision of the story world. However, it usually involves a character other than the protagonist, even though the protagonist may appear as a supporting actor.

Subplots complicate the plot. They also provide alternative interests, sometimes contrasting with the mood of the plot and providing relief. They help to build the world that also holds the plot, and while a subplot may be about something different from the main plotline, it can also add to the plotline, weaving in stories of other characters' lives. Think of your novel as a web of little stories, sometimes crossing, sometimes not. You don't want mini stories that don't seem relevant. You don't want subplots that take up more space than the plot. But a subplot can give the reader another view of the protagonist (as well as the character whose story is the subplot), a friend to lean on, or a colleague to avoid.

3. Write a brief summary of your protagonist's fate and explain how it fulfills your vision for the novel.

Tell your protagonist's story without all the details. Where was he at the beginning of the story, and where is he at the end? How much of what happened was his responsibility? How much was the result of forces greater than he could control? Does the outcome—the place where he is at the end—seem inevitable, given all that has happened? How does the story leave the reader, emotionally?

In a novel of plot, inevitability arises from your milieu, your vision of a world (John le Carré novels). In a novel of character, inevitability arises from who the character is, and whether, in your vision, a person can change (Jane Austen's *Emma*) or whether fate and outside forces are greater than character even at its best (Thomas Hardy's *Tess of the D'Urbervilles*).

Go back and reread your statement of aboutness and assess whether the story proved those things true. If you don't have the feeling of things falling into place perfectly, start taking them apart one by one: the subject, the intention, the context, and so on, testing the events against the vision you had. Try to find what element is out of line, because you will need to make adjustments in plot or structure so that all those chapters add up to the "sum of the story":

This is how it was.
This is what happened.
This is how a problem was solved.
This is how a person's life changed.

Core Scenes

4. Develop a scheme of core scenes.

Unless your novel is exceptionally long, you should be able to see the arc of the story in six to ten major scenes. Start with six; it will force you to evaluate your story. If you have a multiplot, multivoice novel, you would look at each strand of it separately, then look at where they converge. If you have a very long novel (say over three hundred manuscript pages), I would do the core scene work for each of the movements, with four to six in the middle section.

The core scenes are those that establish the key moments in the forward movement of the story; they are developed around major events that result in changes, complications, new situations. They comprise the plot. They vibrate with tension and emotion. The protagonist is in trouble, has to make a decision, reaches out for help, struggles to escape or vanquish, turns a corner. These scenes have to happen for the story to happen. When a reader remembers the book months later, she remembers these scenes. *All core scenes include your protagonist.*

For each scene:

1. Write a caption (abbreviated summary).
2. Identify the setting.

3. State the key event. (What is the source of tension? Is a clock ticking?)
4. State the bull's-eye (the most important moment in the scene, where things take off or explode or collapse or—?).
5. Sum up the emotional state of the protagonist.
6. State the outcome ("how things are at the end").

Why do you think the scene is memorable?

If you do this on index cards or across a large piece of paper, you can look at your story all at once. Read the captions for all the scenes. Then you can consider these questions:

1. Is there an escalation of mystery, need, and tension? *What must happen?*
2. Are the settings the same or different? What do you think of them now? Is there a logic to the choice of settings?
3. Put the captions on a timeline. Could these events unfold closer together? What would have to happen in between? Is there a logic to the time frame?
4. In which scene does the protagonist try the hardest to solve his problem? Why?
5. In which scene does the protagonist have the least hope? Are we on his side?
6. What turning points occur in these scenes? Things like:
   Something is revealed.
   Something is lost.
   There is a power shift.
   The stakes go up.
   The protagonist thinks he can't go on.
   Hope turns to possibility.
   There is a great stillness, and an echo.

   Caption your turning points in a way similar to these statements.

7. Which scenes have strong expression of the protagonist's state of mind, emotions, desires, fears, etc.? What internal conflicts are explored?

Is there a way to heighten any of the effects of the scenes?

What scene is most powerful? Does it create a big turn in the plot? Or solve a big problem?

Look across the scenes. Is there variety in the pace and energy of the scenes?

Now you want to review the scenes you selected and see if you really need them all. If one of them is all about having something happen so that you can convey information—maybe that could be conveyed in summary in another scene. If one of them feels "flat," maybe it isn't dramatic enough to be a scene. Again, you can extract what you need and find a way to fold it into an adjacent passage. On one hand, you want to be economical: Don't have an overlong scene, and don't have a scene at all if it isn't dramatic. On the other hand, the scene is where you can *show* a character in need or jeopardy or struggle or happy arrival.

If you have questions about a scene, look at the one before it and the one after it. (You'll need to go to your manuscript; I'm referring to contiguous scenes, not the prior core scene.) Maybe you have diluted the power of an event by breaking it up. Maybe you have something happening that doesn't have sufficient ground developed in earlier scenes.

If you think every scene is perfect, your next step is to look at it as *the scene after* and *the scene before*, so that either you have an arc in the progression or clearly one of the scenes begins or ends an arc. In other words, you want to see where the scene you have identified as a core scene fits into a sequence of scenes. (You may want to review the example of scene sequences in the section "A Close Look," step #6, "Create timelines for foreground and backstory chronology.")

Fuss with these scenes for a while. Make changes if you think you must. Work in summaries.

For each scene, choose a moment that captures the essence of what has occurred. Imagine yourself taking a photograph. Describe what you see. You want the "photograph" to capture the relationships, the emotion, the sense of tension or release (depending on the moment you chose). Do the six "photos" make an interesting set? For each one, consider whether it is fully felt in the scene as it is written. You may have identified a need for heightened emotion or drama; if so, tag the scene for later revision. Consider what happens in the moment *before the photograph*; consider what happens in the moment *after the photograph*. Now think, again, of the prior and subsequent scenes for each of the six scenes as part of a set. It is most likely that a core scene is the culmination of a sequence, and the scene following it begins a new sequence. If this is not so, look not just at the scene but at the prior and subsequent *sequences*.

Once you have six to ten solid scenes that make up a map of the main action of the novel, you can lay them out horizontally, and then you can create maps between each pair; that's where you sum up the steps it takes to get from Scene 2 to 3, and so on. These are your scene sequences. They are the steps of events or actions that bridge the major scenes. It's like putting up the walls after you've done the framing of a house. Look at your foreground timeline; you may need to fiddle with it, in light of this work on core scenes. Then you create a sequence of scenes between each event; it may take two or three of these sets to comprise the sequence for a "core scene to core scene" plan.

If you've got a big story, this might take a lot of notes, but it must be done. You must, by this point, start to "see" your book in front of you. You will see that there are missing scenes. You will see where you have repeated yourself in either action or emotional outcome. Besides, there is a huge relief in seeing the piles and piles you have produced organized into a logical, manageable, nifty scheme to guide the revision. You can lay the scheme out on a big sheet of newsprint or other paper; and/or you can create index card sets for each scene sequence. Paper-clip sets with front cards that clearly label what each one is.

If your manuscript is heavy with narrative summary and commentary, so much so that you feel the layout of scene sequences doesn't aptly represent the flow of the story, you should make cards to represent the auxiliary (nonscene) elements of your narrative, and attach them to the appropriate sequence. You would sum each passage up according to the function it serves for the story, such as:

- ❏ history of marriage after the baby was born
- ❏ reflections on motherhood
- ❏ analysis of the conflict going on in the detective department
- ❏ meaning of the Dutch painting in the family
- ❏ description of an English garden
- ❏ summary of the aftermath of the student strike

You should be able to storyboard the novel now. See the Resources section for a description of this process.

Lines of Threads

5. Develop a scheme of lines of threads.

What are "threads"?

They are lines of action and meaning that run through the story.

But didn't we just do that with plot and subplots?

Well, yes, but there are other ways to think of them.

What **questions** are raised that the story answers?

What **motifs** throughout the manuscript enrich meaning?

What are the major **emotional issues** in the story interiority?

What elements of **backstory** illuminate the story?

How does **setting** strengthen story?

At this point in your analysis, the most important consideration is what questions are raised, and when, in our story. These are your lines of *plot* and *subplot*.

Make notes if you have ideas about the other lines of threads. You will come back to these as one of your last revision tasks.

QUESTIONS

Read your first forty pages. Every time a question is raised, write it down. If it is answered in those forty pages, put the page number where it was resolved. Most questions will remain open that early in the manuscript.

Let's look at Christopher John Francis Boone (*The Curious Incident of the Dog in the Night-Time*) and the dead poodle, Wellington.

Can Christopher identify the killer? (This is, of course, the line of considerable action and musing.)

Christopher is arrested. *Will he be blamed for the killing?* (Quickly answered no.) This is a very short line in the plot.

Why is Christopher's father so upset (angry, crying, etc.)? The quest to answer this turns up information about Christopher's parents—his mother is alive, though he was told she was dead—and adds a major subplot.

How will the father handle this turn of events? (He hits Christopher hard enough to knock him out.)

His father admits to killing Wellington. But by now we have the second plotline: Christopher wants to find his mother.

Can Christopher navigate a journey to London?
Will his mother want him?

Every question is the canopy for a sequence of events. Christopher making his way to London, for example, involves challenges such as overcoming his claustrophobia in a busy train; navigating a city station; finding his mother's flat, etc.

And by then we have a new question: *Will Christopher's father and mother be able to come to terms with their history (both had affairs)? How will the family sort out an arrangement for Christopher to have both parents?*

And all along there has been this question: *Will Christopher pass his A-level exam in math?*

At first, the plot of this novel sounds simple. But because of Christopher's special abilities and limitations, it is quite complicated. And the most interesting thing about the story is how Christopher solves problem after problem, going through experiences of paralyzing fear, confusion, determination, analysis, invention, and so on. His voice, his explanation, and his feelings—though he claims to have no feelings—are fascinating and engaging. For all along, it turns out, Christopher has been writing a book, this book, about his quest, and so he has a lot to say about what happens and how he solves the mystery of the dog, sets in motion the meeting of his estranged parents, adjusts to a new way of living, and conveys it all, by writing it down.

To understand the structure of the book you would need to list the questions raised and then the line of action that answers each. You would also need to list all the ways that Christopher makes special adjustments, his very own strategies, for accomplishing what he does. I would call those adjustments "motifs" in our analysis. So your line of threads would look something like this:

story question → actions that lead to answer →
character's special adjustments

MOTIFS: Ideas or devices that recur

Madame Bovary, as you would expect, is chock-full of motifs. I think right at the top is *lies*. Emma's whole life is a lie, sometimes because she doesn't understand the truth, sometimes because she can't admit it, sometimes because she feels she must hide it.

There are numerous references to sickness and death, so many that you wonder if Flaubert wasn't a bit morbid. So many things decay: potatoes, legs, the skin of a beggar. I'm sure Flaubert saw this as being realistic. And every reference to death or dissolution is a step toward the inevitable death of poor Emma.

In *All the Pretty Horses* horses matter to Grady, the protagonist, as much or more than people. He talks to his horse. He wishes humans could be like horses. He trains horses. And there is blood. Men are shot. Horses bleed. Grady bleeds. His lover bites his hand and draws blood. So much in this novel is about being a man, a westerner, a cowboy: prevailing, bearing up stoically. There are many kinds of pain.

I don't think you plan motifs, at least not at first. They rise to the surface as you write the story. You are reviewing your manuscript and they pop up at you. Then you can exploit them. Suddenly you realize that every door seems to get slammed shut; that boys without fathers get into trouble; that photographs can be sentimental but also cruel; that cars are thrilling but also dangerous. You see that characters come bearing gifts but they get cast aside.

Certain things come up again and again; in revision, you watch for them, you consider their effect, you emphasize or mute their appearance. You don't want to hit the reader over the head, but repetition echoes through a story. Look for echoes in yours.

EMOTIONAL ISSUES

Study your passages of interiority. What issues come up again and again with your protagonist? Sure, there will be reactions to what is going on, what she wants. But what is she afraid of? What haunts her? Look beneath her behavior for things she doesn't say. Know what she would never ever do, but does.

BACKSTORY

Closely allied to emotional issues, obviously, are events in the past that still resonate for a character. In revision, you want to edit backstory. Is it crowded by too many memories of different things? Could they be compressed so that one event, or one trait of a character, or even one thing that Mother always said, gets repeated, and proven?

In *Walking Dunes*, David thinks about his parents' history. His father, a New York Jew, met his mother, a West Texas nurse, during the war in a New York hospital. They moved back to Texas, and something about that has always troubled David—the sense that his mother made the choice of how he, David, would be raised. That his father let himself cede power to David's mother. David is afraid and perhaps contemptuous of this idea, and it matters to him that his own future gets tied up with a pretty girl who loves him and is his link to a better life. Are all men users or losers? Do women hold the power?

In *Plain Seeing*, Lucy can't get over her mother's death. She feels cheated. She feels as if her mother died just when she was most needed (Lucy was a teenager). How could Lucy know how to be a woman? How could Lucy know if she was making her mother's mistakes?

SETTING

There is immense power in *where*.

Geography is paramount in *The Great Gatsby*. East Egg and West Egg are contrasting representations of two kinds of wealth: inherited, "classy," aristocratic rich versus flashy new rich. There is also the contrast of the immoral East to the solid values of the West. Weather is exploited, too, with pouring rain and scorching sun.

In *All the Pretty Horses*, it's all about geography. John Grady has left Texas behind for what he thinks is a true West, a place where he can be a cowboy—a man of virtue and skill. He encounters fierce blasts of weather, the long vistas of terrain, and the beauty of a prosperous ranch. But Mexico isn't his place, and he is forced to leave it. McCarthy's descriptions of the landscape are vivid and violent and precise and poetic.

As I said before, another consideration—besides choosing settings that evoke powerful connections to emotions—is variety. You don't want to be everywhere, but you also don't want to be boring. Try to think of setting not only as a place, but as a place where certain things are true, and certain things happen. Let your event be part of that inevitability, *or* let your event contradict expectations. A young couple take a picnic to an idyllic spot, but a fierce wind comes up, blowing away their cloth and sending their lunch tumbling. So what? What better place for them to embrace, to express their love that cannot be assailed?

There should be places in your story that mean something; those are the settings for major events. From setting can come interruptions, solace, harassment, harmony, danger. As you work through your manuscript, think about every single scene's setting to be sure you have exploited the possibilities, that you are not choosing the boring default site. And keep in mind that although you probably don't want to spend a lot of words on description, choose the words you do use carefully. Wherever you can be precise about a tree, a plant, a sky, a room, a window, you build believability and texture.

EXERCISES

❏ Choose a scene in your manuscript at random. Identify the thread—the line of action or meaning—that *comes from or leads into* another scene or chapter. The second instance of the thread may not be in the scene immediately following, but you should recognize threads and be able to look forward or backward in the manuscript to connect them.

When was the thread introduced, and how? This is your initiating event of a line of meaning that appears again.

Where does it logically reach some kind of end? (It may not be the end of the book.)

❏ Choose a plot point late in the manuscript where something important happens. Now plot backward in steps until you come to the scene where you can see that the seed was planted for its outcome at that later point where you started the analysis. Identify the "interruptions" to the line of action or theme, and consider whether there is too much space between scenes that develop it.

You want to have several strong threads that pull through the manuscript, but you don't want so many that they become confusing or intrusive. Subplots should increase engagement and tension, not excessively interrupt the ongoing dramatic line.

6. Identify key scene sequences in each plot movement.

These do not make up *all* the scenes; you are choosing your strongest sets.

You probably have already done a lot of work with scene sequences, if you followed my suggestions in the section on core scenes. Here, though, start by isolating three key sequences, one for each movement. It's likely that the first one will come some time after you introduce the problem. It's more difficult to pin down what's most important in the rest of the book. But pointing your finger and saying *Here's where I'm putting my money* makes you deal with structure (how the story is organized) and meaning (what it adds up to) in very specific ways. A sequence by definition is made up of one thing following another, so you want those steps in the sequence to have pace and rhythm and an undercurrent of feeling. If scenes "belong together" in that they build from one situation to the next, you have to look at what (if anything) comes between them. If, for example, between a first and second scene you employ a long passage of backstory, be sure to evaluate how you bring the reader back to the business of the line of action.

You are trying to identify where it is in your manuscript that things happen in the most interesting, most forward-motion way. Once you have done that—named three sequences—you can look at your other sets of scenes, the ways that you link plot points. Unless you are writing a thriller, you don't want a constant drumbeat of action. You want sequences that have scenes of respite, interstices of response and commentary, gentler movement. You want variety. Don't worry about writing those sequences quite yet.

It is possible that this will be a difficult undertaking. I often see manuscripts that don't organize scenes into sets or sequences. Scenes are, instead, strung out like beads on a slack cord. If you see that yours are related like that, try to make the line taut, bring the scenes closer together, and be more deliberate about where the breaks between lines of action take place.

This analysis will help you handle the tension in the manuscript, and also help you find the best places to let the story sink into its history or meaning in passages of interiority or commentary. Reviewing your lines of threads will help you balance scene and response.

7. Identify passages, scenes, and chapters from the first draft that will be used in the revision.

Remember what you have at this point:

1. Your original manuscript, with the many notes you made and exercises you did.
2. Your summaries of the three movements of the novel.
3. Your major scene sequence for each movement.

You will need to fill in the rest of the scene sequences later, but first, look at your original manuscript and decide what you can use in your revision as is or slightly revised, and what you can't.

It will help if you have a page that lists your core scenes in front of you, and your three scene sequences (for the three movements) handy for reference. It's like a map as you look back over your bound manuscript. You are looking for the writing that is basically solid and can be transferred to the revised draft. As you decide on such a chapter, go to your loose pages and put them, paper-clipped, into a stack. Call it "Yes" or whatever pleases you. This doesn't mean perfect passages. It means passages that are substantially sufficient. You will critique each as you come to it and write to improve it if necessary, but these are parts of the manuscript that "fit" and do what you want them to do. Hurrah! I've been known to put on lipstick and kiss the first page of such a chapter.

Right now, you need to survey the manuscript to see what proportion of it is fairly solid.

8. Identify passages, scenes, and chapters that need new drafts.

It is possible that your concept of your novel has changed so much in your analysis that what you have now is a broad summary of a new version; you should also have the summaries and scene sequences of the three movements of the story. It is likely that you will have much that you can use.

Also, this is a good time to be especially alert for weak or tangled complications. You want the problems in the story to be tightly related, to escalate the reader's concern for the protagonist, and to give opportunity for passages of deep interiority.

Deciding what needs to be rewritten may be a matter of choosing a scene or a whole chapter that just does not work, knowing that you will have to take it apart and start over from the crumbs. Or it may be a matter of recognizing the essential function of the scene or chapter and not liking the way it is shaped and developed. Either way, when you pick it up for revision, you will read it, think about what strengths can feed your rewrite, and then write from scratch. No filling in holes, no borrowing nice phrases. An organic, coherent, flowing new passage.

If the selected passage has a lot of notes on it from the work you've done as you passed through these pages, stop now and sum up your critique, write it out, and attach it to the front of the chapter from the loose pages. You want to be able to pick it back up later and know whether you are revising an essentially adequate chapter, or if you are going to replace it. If you come to a chapter with a scene you definitely aren't going to use, block it out with a felt marker and make a note, but keep stacking the manuscript so you have things in order. When you identify a section you know you aren't going to use, mark it to indicate whether you are deleting it entirely or replacing it. You may have notes from your many exercises, and you can attach or tape them to pages and insert them where they are relevant.

Keep the loose pages (caught in scenes or chapters with paper clips) together in sequence, separate from the chapters that you think you can use in the revision more or less as is.

So now you have two stacks:

1. Scenes and chapters you can use, with some work.
2. Scenes and chapters you don't think you can use (but you might want to look at again).

You also have your summaries and your scene sequences.

If you have a gush of inspiration now, by all means write, but if you feel very much in the analysis mode, set the pages aside and keep going.

9. Decide whether you will amend your first draft or begin again with a new manuscript.

This is a big decision and it is hard to make a general recommendation. If you see problems (or, perhaps a better way to think of it, possibilities) in just about every chapter; if you see a way to up the energy and power of the story; if you want to take the story to a new plane; start with the first page and write. This can be energizing, productive, and, ultimately, the most efficient way to proceed.

This doesn't mean you have to "start all over," although you might want to. You have all these notes, all this work, the ideas, the scenes. You have been developing a section-by-section guide of scene sequences, which you can complete before you begin writing a new draft. You can annotate the section guide with references to the old passages you should reread as you come to those chapters. Back and forth, old and new, you bring the history of your dream with you into its new version. All the work you did in the first draft; all the work you did in exercises; all the work you've done in this stage ("The Plan"): You draw on the material as you progress through an orderly start-to-finish reshaping or rewriting. That's a revision.

Be very wary of cut-and-paste. Even if you know you are going to use "these two pages," retyping them provides the necessary bridge from two new passages, and even if you change only a few words, take out a sentence or two, it will help you maintain coherence and flow.

I urge you to create a new, orderly overview of the novel made up of these items:

1. Your foreground timeline, identifying key events.
2. A summary of the novel.
3. Separate summaries of the three parts of the novel.
4. Scene sequences organized in sets, key event to key event.
5. Scene sequences organized into chapters, with taglines.

A note from ancient days: All my novels were written on a typewriter, so there wasn't any way for me *not* to rewrite, and my experience was that even if I thought I had a great chapter, once I got to retyping it into the new manuscript, I made some amendments.

I also found that index cards worked well for me because I could key them to old chapters and pages, and look back at the old draft as a reminder, but use the cards to guide me in the new writing. I guess what I'm saying is, don't let your computer do too much of your revising for you. One way or another, as you do a revised draft, you have to enter it in a new file, page by page. That helps you maintain the voice of the story consistently. It gives you flow.

Don't rush. Don't dawdle. Don't doubt.

10. Write a document that describes your love of your story.

Reflect on the work you have done and all you have accomplished. Restate your resolution. Respect the process that is taking you forward.

Don't skip this step!

Consider the questions I raised earlier, in the section on the novel continuum.

Does the *idea of the story* seem fresh? If you have even the slightest uneasiness that a cliché is lurking, weed it out. Your tools: *What if? What else?* Often all it takes is a twist in one character trait, one plot point, to brighten your story.

Is the story line well constructed? Does it come together satisfactorily—but not too early? Is it predictable or surprising?

Is there someone to love?

Is there something to fear?

Does someone grow up?

Do you hear a storyteller's voice in your telling?

Could something be louder, quieter, stronger, scarier, more loving, more alone, *more important*? Why not make it so?

Consider these issues, and if something nags at you, use it as a starting point for reconsidering elements of the story as you review your notes. Maybe walk away for a week. When you come back, you may think you were just being negative. Or you may be able to put your finger on a fault line and fix it.

Three: The Process

Warm up

If you haven't done some of the exercises yet, this would be a good time to look at them. Generating new material from prompts gets you in a fresh frame of mind and gives you more to draw from in revision.

1. Review or generate new material. Give yourself time to experiment: Rewrite a section from a different POV. Open the novel in a different place on the timeline. Use a different narrative strategy. Identify new plot points. Adjust your outline.
2. Fine-tune your premise (statement of aboutness). Write a two- or three-sentence description you might show to a reader, agent, or editor. Make a "premise banner" and put it on the wall.
3. Write jacket copy or back copy for the novel. Write a dream review.

1. *Review or generate new material.* As you rewrite passages, tuck them in with the draft chapters. Don't worry right now about fit and transition. Don't pull away because you see yourself going in a new direction—you can always turn back later. Don't be afraid of pushing your vision, your inventiveness, your emotions. Choose points in the story where you have deep feelings, or you want to solve a puzzle or try out a new idea. You may write a new scene 150 pages in that gives you a whole new vision.

2. *Fine-tune your premise (statement of aboutness).* I promise you, everyone finds this to be a tough assignment. It might take you twenty tries to get a statement you can show someone. You have been working on this throughout the book. You've seen your statement evolve. Working on it has always been about giving yourself a beacon, a guide. Now consider if you have a statement yet that is ready for prime time: sharing it with a fellow writer, showing it to an editor or agent. You want the statement to represent exactly what you believe you have written (will write?). You want it to grab a reader. You want to think of it in the New Reads section of your favorite magazine. *One more time.*

3. *Write jacket copy or back copy for the novel.* Before you write jacket copy or a review, read a lot of examples. Look at what the "flap copy" (the description that begins on the left flap of a hardcover book's jacket) accomplishes—how it draws you in as a reader without giving too much away. I've always written flap copy and put it in front of my manuscript. It helps my agent talk about the book; it helps an editor talk about it to colleagues; it helps publicists. Nobody expects this from you, but if you feel confident and excited about writing it, why not pass it along? And for right now, it helps you pin your story down to its essence.

Then look at how people "blurb" one another. What do you wish someone would say about your book? Or (my preference) look at paperback reprints, where there are often passages about the book that replace front flap copy (there's no front flap), but are usually a little shorter. What do you think would pull a reader in?

Read reviews to see what gets talked about, what makes reviewers carp or praise. See what reviewers have said about books you've read and whether you agree. Then imagine what someone might write about your story. Someone who "got it." Don't be shy.

Revise

1. Write a new summary of the novel without reviewing old versions. Compare your various summaries and refine the latest one. Expand into three summaries, one for each movement of the novel (beginning, middle, end). This is your guide for revision.
2. Develop your outline: a section-by-section guide. Write scenarios of chapters. Write beat sheets for scene sequences.
3. Review the passages, scenes, and chapters from the first draft that you will use in the revision. Annotate for needed adjustments. Insert notes for new scenes and chapters.
4. Spell out your strategy for tackling the revision. Establish a calendar and schedule. Plan for breaks and rewards.
5. Rewrite the first chapter.
6. Write new chapters nested in the sequence of the manuscript.

1. Write a new summary of the novel without reviewing old versions. Compare your various summaries and refine the latest one. Expand into three summaries, one for each movement of the novel (beginning, middle, end). This is your guide for revision.

Review and perhaps revise your foreground timeline.

You know about summaries by now, so do it. This is the flow of the story, compressed. Not the details, not the descriptions, just the pure resonance of Story. This should be exciting and affirming.

2. Develop your outline: a section-by-section guide. Write taglines and scenarios of chapters. Then write beat sheets for scene sequences within chapters.

   A beat sheet specifies dramatic action, narrative summary, and backstory references.

   You need to spell out the scene sequences for the whole novel. You may want to wait to write the beat sheets as you approach each chapter, but you should write all the chapter summaries before you begin writing.

   Develop this guide tidily. It is your outline, a condensed version of the novel. If you have thought through all of the action of the plot, in steps, you will be able to focus on the writing itself. You will be immersed in the dream you have created.

IF YOU HAVE done all the exercises up to this point, this will be mostly a matter of reviewing your work and pulling it together, then typing it up and printing it out.

Within each movement, there are sets of scenes that make up an arc of the plot. Write a brief summary of what each sequence accomplishes for the story. Then write a very brief caption of each scene (titles or sentences). Group these captions into sets for the sequences. Note that you are looking at the dramatic elements of the story at this point. This makes up a beat sheet (record of steps) in your scene sequence.

If a scene sequence includes substantial narrative summary (a bridge between scenes that is compressed), note it as part of the beat sheet with the notation **NS** (narrative summary). Likewise, if there is significant backstory (not included within a scene), note it, too, on your beat sheet, as **BS** (backstory). Backstory should also be captioned or titled. Ultimately, all of the major components of your chapters should be identified.

When you are ready to write, you will need to have this close look at the pieces of the story, but you will also need the more global view of the story proceeding chapter by chapter. So now organize your sequence summaries into chapters, and *write a brief summary of each chapter. Now write taglines for each chapter. Post the taglines where you can look at them as you write.*

Read your taglines straight through. This is an overview of your novel. Read your chapter summaries straight through. This is your story. You have made tremendous progress not only in identifying and understanding your story, but in organizing its parts. When you do the actual writing in revising, you can concentrate on *writing*, not on making up new stuff, not on figuring out what needs to happen next, not on what the character is feeling here, not on what you need to explain.

Now, with your outline at hand:

3. Review the passages, scenes, and chapters from the first draft that you will use in the revision. Annotate for needed adjustments. Insert notes for new scenes and chapters.

    You should now have a "bundle" of the loose pages, arranged in chunks of chapters, perhaps with different colors of paper. You also have a lot of notes on the backs of pages in your bound copy.

4. Spell out your strategy for tackling the revision. Establish a calendar and schedule. Plan for breaks and rewards.

    Figure out how you are going to transfer notes from the bound copy and from the index card sequences you created to your loose pages. I would definitely use a different color of paper, transfer notes neatly, attach them where they are relevant. Or you can transfer notes as you come to each chapter. Keep your outline (from step 2 above) separate. If you can post it some way, all the better. Have some kind of system that tracks what you haven't picked up yet, what you are working on, and what you have processed. Piles get shuffled.

You are going to have to fiddle with what you have produced and organize it in a way that makes sense to you. I've given you a start but there are so many variables, book to book and person to person. I just know planning involves a lot of paper and colors and cards, and not just your laptop at the coffee shop. Once you start revising, however, you can pick up a chapter at a time.

I do know that Anne Lamott had it right when she admonished the writer to proceed "bird by bird," as her father had once advised her younger brother while he was undertaking a daunting school report about birds. You can't do everything at once. And you can't shrivel with fear thinking about the challenges ahead. You have to do the task in front of you, and then the next one. You'll get there by sheer doggedness. Perseverance is the best friend of talent.

5. Rewrite the first chapter.

Let's assume for a moment that you are perfectly happy with your first chapter. I would still type it out again. Who knows what little gifts of phrases or insights may fly in? And if indeed it's perfect, and you type it with a little bit of annoyance and a larger bit of satisfaction, you are entering your revision from your strength.

And if you need to write a new chapter, you have so much to build on now. You know what the story will be and how you will tell it. This is you turning on the lights.

Have you established a *tone* for your book, something that distinguishes your voice and the feeling of the novel? (Read lots of openings!!) What promises have you made the reader? That this story will be light and fun? That it will be deeply emotional and concerned with important themes? That it will transport the reader to an unusual time and place?

6. Write new chapters nested in the sequence of the manuscript.

You must follow your own instincts here.

I'm inclined to say, review your core scenes first, not even necessarily the whole chapters. You should have them in mind clearly. Then I'd see what your notes tell you about making changes, and keep moving forward from now on. You'll feel that you have things so chopped up that it worries you—*Can I keep track of all this?* So following your outline, your scene sequences, and your piles of pages and notes is a logical way to proceed. Solve the problem in front of you. If it means yet another slight change in something later, you'll know it when you get to it. And all along, you want the feeling of following the story, not jumping around.

What I want to think is that you will move with a steady pace, not rushing, but not suffering, either. *You know your story.* Tell it.

Write your revised draft steadily, confidently, alternating preparation and review with your writing and rewriting.

Four: The Polish

Now confident in your story, structure, and strategy, edit for economy, focus, and grace

This is the time when I would go through the manuscript again, looking for and touching up motifs. You will already have them in your manuscript; this is a refinement step. The first step is to thumb through your pages specifically looking for images that recur, perhaps to your surprise. In Edwidge Danticat's novel *Breath, Eyes, Memory*, there are powerful recurring images of pain and blood, lies and betrayal, mothers and daughters. See what has arisen from your story, and be sure you have exploited it, if it supports your themes. Think of the heat, light, and aridity in Paul Bowles's *The Sheltering Sky*. Look for the ways you have established a sense of place, and see if something from early in the book could reappear later, and mean more because of the accrual of events. Reread the section "Describe the world of the novel," in "Stage One: A Close Look," and decide if you've done so to your satisfaction.

Comb your story for places where you tried to engage the reader's senses viscerally, calling up smells or sounds, for example. Assess whether you have effectively used specific details. You'll want to attend to this in the scenes that carry a lot of weight. Smaller scenes, transition scenes, abbreviations of action, and so on, don't need this kind of close brushwork. But sometimes the light on a polished table or the smell of decaying roses can enhance emotional effects because they reflect the essence of what is happening.

Open your manuscript at random four or five times and read a couple of pages. Ask yourself: Do these scenes reflect time and place? You don't want your novel to feel generic, a story that could happen in Texas as easily as in Rhode Island, in winter as well as in spring. What is the mood of this scene? Oh yeah? What words and phrases make it so?

Consider the pace of your novel. Choose a scene that is meant to move right along—things happen, something changes. Does it? How so? Is the dialogue crisp? Are sentences shorter than in other chapters? Do incidents clang against one another? Or could you trim, compress, and accelerate the action? Perhaps eliminate unneeded description. If, for example, events have spiraled to a point of reversal or revelation, and your character is socked in the gut and can go no further, does the pace reflect his emotional state? Does he think about what has happened? Does the reader have a chance to *feel*?

Review your core scenes yet again. Is there energy in them that pulls you into the action? Are there places where you can sink into the heart of the protagonist, feel what she is feeling, ache for her?

PAGE THROUGH THE book and write captions of five "caught moments" that could be photographs. What is it about those moments that is captivating? Beautiful? Ugly? Provocative? Does the passage truly convey what you see in the characters at that moment? Readers should have a few strong memories from the book. Images. Feelings. Something a character said. A moment of tension, surprise, or joy. Can you make them more memorable? Imagine yourself drawing a box around "that moment." How do your words accomplish this? *Here, dear reader, remember this.*

Ask yourself: If I were the reader talking to a friend, how would I finish this sentence: "I'll never forget . . ."

LOOK FOR EVERY extraneous word and take it out. And here's a challenge for you: Circle all your adverbs. Then decide if you really want them to remain. Mark all sentences that start with *-ing* phrases: "Crying out in pain, she stumbled to the chair." "Hating him with all her heart, she stomped away." "Putting the laundry away, they made sandwiches and watched TV." (That last one's from a real manuscript!)

Look at every place you have replaced "said" with alternatives like "stuttered," "whispered," "shouted," and change most if not all back to "said."

How much of this work do you do? As much as you can.

Problems with diction, sentence structure, dialogue, and other fine points of style and correctness are outside the scope of this guide. You may need to work with another book to improve your sentences. You may need to review grammar. In the Resources section I've listed some excellent books to help you. Ultimately, you may need a copy editor, too.

Maybe a writer friend will read your manuscript, looking for any infelicities. Mostly, take the time, yourself, to look again. If you have some sort of writing glitch, name it and do something about it. If you are in some way dyslexic, to take another example, plan to have someone review the manuscript before you give it to someone who will evaluate it. (I have a friend—a good writer—who cannot master homophones. She doesn't see her inevitable errors: mane for main; shear for sheer; great for grate, etc. It is a form of dyslexia. So I read her final manuscript and correct them all. She has published five mysteries.)

Read through the manuscript by reading only the first page of each chapter. Do you feel excited by the pages? Or do you hear yourself repeating strategies, or taking too long to get things going? Rework what is slow, boring, confusing, or overly familiar. Make the first paragraph of each chapter a jewel.

Approach your revised manuscript with great respect and affection and the desire for every line to say what you mean for it to say, as nicely as possible. I have one special piece of advice: Read every sentence aloud. Move it around in your mouth. Don't let your sentences get tangled; when in doubt, break them up. Strive for utmost clarity. Transparency is underrated: If you aren't calling attention to yourself, you *are* calling attention to the *story*. I don't know any better way to raise a writer's consciousness than to read aloud.

Line to line. Paragraph to paragraph. Page to page.

All the way to the end.

THERE ARE NO rules for novels, save this: *Engage the reader.* From that flows everything else—all our considerations of subject and style, sufficiency and shape. For direction, go to your heart. For instruction, go to novels themselves. The work of describing texts builds a repertoire of strategies for writing. Think next of process, map out possible strategies. Consider the mountain you would climb.

I wish you well.

P.S. Save everything for your archives.

Resources

Recommended Books on Craft

Douglas Bauer. *The Stuff of Fiction: Advice on Craft.* This isn't nuts and bolts. It's a deep reflection on essential elements of fiction: dialogue, dramatic events, closings, etc. Readable, practical, thoughtful.

Charles Baxter. *The Art of Subtext: Beyond Plot.* Not for the faint of heart, but Baxter is a joy to read, and his discussion of the hidden overtones and undertones in fiction will raise the bar for your writing.

Renni Browne and Dave King. *Self-Editing for Fiction Writers: How to Edit Yourself into Print.* Practical, down-to-earth, basic. If you're still shaky about things like point of view, interior monologue, and dialogue mechanics, this is the book for you.

William Cane. *Fiction Writing Master Class: Emulating the Work of Great Novelists to Master the Fundamentals of Craft.* If you like the idea of learning from the likes of Hemingway, Wharton, Melville, and Margaret Mitchell, this book is fun and smart. How did Faulkner use mystery? How did Ian Fleming exploit details? How did Philip K. Dick write such good dialogue?

Claire Kehrwald Cook. *Line by Line: How to Edit Your Own Writing*. An MLA editor, Cook knows where the glitches are, the ones you might miss, especially with sentence craft. A very smart book.

Constance Hale. *Sin and Syntax: How to Craft Wicked Good Prose*. Readable, jazzy, and practical. Don't underestimate the power of your diction. Don't underestimate the challenge of rising to it.

John Hough, Jr. *The Fiction Writer's Guide to Dialogue: A Fresh Look at an Essential Ingredient of the Craft*. You'll know if you need this. The book is an outstanding guide to the basics of constructing dialogue as well as issues of integrating dialogue into plot. I like the high quality of choices of models. Hough has helpful things to say about the uses of vernacular and indirect discourse. Dialogue is a great big elephant when you don't have control of it. Be sure you do. The visual artist learns perspective and values; the musician practices scales; you conquer punctuation and dialogue.

David Jauss. "From Long Shots to X-Rays: Distance and Point of View in Fiction," in *Alone with All That Could Happen: Re-thinking Conventional Wisdom about the Craft of Fiction Writing*. An excellent discussion of point-of-view options and how your choice affects your story. The book is a collection of Jauss's craft essays, and all of them are excellent.

Alice Kaplan. *Looking for the Stranger: Albert Camus and the Life of a Literary Classic*. Like a million other college students, I had to translate *The Stranger* from the French. I fell in love, and I've read the book many times. What's exciting and informative about Kaplan's book is that she gives us a kind of biography of the novel itself: how it was born and grew. She shows how Camus got ideas, and sometimes specific utterances, from his work as a crime reporter, for example. She finds the seeds of the novel in early writings. She draws on his diaries and letters. She makes a reader understand how Camus found his character's unforgettable first-person voice.

She illustrates how a novel must come into meaning and form for the writer.

Stephen Koch. *The Modern Library Writer's Workshop: A Guide to the Craft of Fiction.* The author, former chair of Columbia University's graduate creative writing program, is the ultimate mentor. If you read only one book, make it this one, and in any case, read it first. Koch's advice about drafts and revision is so right on I am always tempted to sit and read the chapters aloud to my students. It's a process. It takes time. He also says great things about character.

Alice LaPlante. *The Making of a Story: A Norton Guide to Creative Writing.* This is a book to start with if you feel the least bit shaky about creative writing. LaPlante explains what's what and the how and the why of all the basics, from the role of concrete details to show and tell, point of view, and so on. She presents information, examples, and exercises. This is a big, smart, friendly book that wraps you up in creative prose craft. It isn't about novel writing, it's about writing story, with lots of models and analyses and straight talk. It's worth the time it takes to study it.

Priscilla Long. *The Writer's Portable Mentor: A Guide to Art, Craft, and the Writing Life.* Whatever you write, this is bound to feel like a friend. More sentence strategies; some interesting ideas about structure; friendly advice about the writing life.

Noah Lukeman. *A Dash of Style: The Art and Mastery of Punctuation.* This little book is a terrific overview of important basic aspects of structure in fiction, with advice about punctuating sentences, dialogue, and, in effect, paragraphs. I require my students to read it and they are always glad they did.

Elizabeth Lyon. *Manuscript Makeover: Revision Techniques No Fiction Writer Can Afford to Ignore.* There is so much good advice in this book, you can't use it all. If you are aiming for a broad general audience, or writing a genre novel, it is especially helpful. Lyon covers a lot of ground. She is also helpful in practical matters: writing synopses and queries, for example.

Donald Maass. *Writing 21st Century Fiction: High-Impact Techniques for Exceptional Storytelling.* This is a great big dunk into contemporary popular novels, with very smart ideas about why readers love them. I'd be derelict not to send you to at least one of Maass's books (any will do, really) for smart advice and a boost of energy. He also has workbooks available; you may find him helpful as you write a first draft or rewrite it before undertaking a revision.

Thomas McCormack. *The Fiction Editor, the Novel, and the Novelist: A Book for Writers, Teachers, Publishers, and Anyone Else Devoted to Fiction.* This is a book for writing geeks. McCormack has a kooky, slightly arrogant way of discussing the role of the editor—and therefore, what needs editing—and he has invented a whole vocabulary for talking about novels. But it's worth it to learn his concepts of "circuitry" and the "master-effect." I found the first edition of this book very early in my career and I felt lights go on when I read it. Besides, it's fun to read him destroy the whole idea of theme.

Robert C. Meredith and John D. Fitzgerald. *Structuring Your Novel: From Basic Idea to Finished Manuscript.* Structure, structure, structure. Fourteen ways. I insist that all my students use this book because it makes them think about *where the story comes from*, about why they are the right writers to tell it, and because it acts as a benevolent organizer. In a world of razzle-dazzle, *Structuring Your Novel* is old-fashioned common sense. And a treasure. Be careful, there's more than one book of this title, so get the right authors.

Jessica Page Morrell. *Between the Lines: Master the Subtle Elements of Fiction Writing.* This is a veritable toolbox of skills to help you create coherence and layers in your novel. Excellent discussions of subplots, transitions, flashbacks.

Paula Munier. *Plot Perfect: Building Unforgettable Stories Scene by Scene.* We are in the same corner, urging writers to create story structure scene by scene. Lots of plotting templates and examples, a good backup. Good advice about sustaining tension.

George Plimpton. *Writers at Work: 6th Series*. Here you will find reflections on craft by Bernard Malamud, Nadine Gordimer, John Gardner, Kurt Vonnegut, Jr., and others. The whole series is mind-bending.

Sandra Scofield. *The Scene Book: A Primer for the Fiction Writer*. I poured everything I thought mattered about writing scenes into it, taking great care to create a basic, solid vocabulary and scheme for analysis. There are dozens of models, closely read, and exercises to set the ideas firmly. There are also templates you can use to study writers you admire *and* to evaluate your own scenes.

Joan Silber. *The Art of Time in Fiction: As Long As It Takes*. "One of the main tasks a writer faces is defining the duration of a plot." Amen. Silber is a brisk, direct, insightful teacher; and she's a wonderful writer, too—read her fiction soon.

Francis Steegmuller. *Flaubert and Madame Bovary: A Double Portrait*. I learned about this biography from reading Stephen Koch's book, and it was worth the whole price. I can't think of any writer who has so meticulously (agonizingly) recorded his steps in writing a novel. I love that it was so important to him to *see* what was happening in the story.

Sarah Stone and Ron Nyren. *Deepening Fiction: A Practical Guide for Intermediate and Advanced Writers*. This isn't a book for beginners, although its discussions of point of view and of the revision process are gold, and you may want to study it. It's meant for intermediate writers, and it's focused on short stories. When I started teaching in MFA programs I spent almost a year working through Stone and Nyren's exercises for myself; it was time well spent.

Lessons from Model Novels

Context and structure in *Number the Stars* by Lois Lowry

This novel for middle grade readers was published in 1989 and has never been out of print. It's a lovely book to read (a good story told well) and a good book to study (with a clean, clear structure). It takes place in 1943 Copenhagen, when the Germans have decided to "relocate" the Jews of Denmark. Only the Danes aren't having it. There is a fierce and effective underground campaign to move the country's Jews, a population of nearly seven thousand people, across the sea to Sweden. This was a long time ago, and most Americans don't know the story, so it's dramatic and powerful for a child—or an adult, for that matter—to read.

Initially, Annemarie Johansen's family has taken in her best friend, Ellen Rosen, whose family lives in the same building. The girls pretend to be sisters—which poses some problems in blond Denmark. Eventually everyone realizes that hiding in plain sight isn't enough, and the Johansens help Ellen's family escape the Germans entirely.

The novel is written in seventeen titled chapters. Each one is a short scene sequence. The passage of time is taken care of in efficient summaries, such as this one at the beginning of chapter 3:

"The days of September passed, one after the other, much the same. Annemarie and Ellen walked to school together, and home again, always now taking the longer way, avoiding the tall soldier and his partner."

Winter has come and there's no fuel. Times are hard for everyone. But the real fear is getting caught, such as when soldiers come to the apartment and ask who the dark-haired sister really is. Meanwhile, Annemarie's brother is helping families get away, across the sea, using a relative's farmhouse as a base of operations. As things become more dangerous, the family realizes that Ellen is in danger, too, and the girls are taken to the countryside, where Ellen is reunited with her family and eventually taken with them by boat to Sweden. Of course there are threats from the Germans, who are always on the lookout for just such schemes.

There is no need for backstory as the story is all about present danger. There is subtext: the pride and courage of the Danish Resistance; the courage of the Jews; the rabid invasion of the German soldiers; the bonds of friendship, loyalty, family, and citizenship. Because the story is told from the girls' viewpoints, much of what is going on can be kept subtle and not frightening, though it is obviously dangerous.

It would be a valuable exercise to take a few of the motifs (named in the paragraph above) and list the references that develop them, chapter to chapter.

The chapters are vivid and engaging. The story moves quickly without high emotion; it is carried by what happens, what people are doing and saying. For this reason, it is a good lesson for a novelist, a reminder that a good story has a strong pulse thumping through every chapter, and characters we care about.

This would be an easy book to storyboard as an introduction to structure.

Chapter openings in *Wolf Hall* by Hilary Mantel

There's so much to admire about Mantel's writing: its liveliness, richness of detail, conciseness, wit, convincing dialogue, respect for the intelligence of the reader. I liked what Wendy Lesser said in *Bookforum* (www.bookforum.com): All her novels "contain the essential Mantel element, which is a style—of writing *and* of thinking—that combines steely-eyed intelligence with intense yet wide-ranging sympathy."

Wolf Hall is set in 1520s England, when Henry VIII is desperate for a male heir. He is ready to cast off Anne Boleyn and try another wife, but it's not so easy to fire a queen. Here comes Thomas Cromwell, and Mantel's brilliant portrait of a complicated, implacable man. It's one of my all-time favorite novels.

But what I want to point out just now is how delightfully Mantel varies her chapter openings. She uses an omniscient point of view—her narration sees everything, knows everything. I'm simply going to give the first paragraph of each of several early chapters to demonstrate how handily she pulls the reader in, how much she accomplishes quickly, and how various is her strategy.

Part One

I. Across the Narrow Sea

"So now get up."

Felled, dazed, silent, he has fallen; knocked full length on the cobbles of the yard. His head turns sideways; his eyes are turned toward the gate, as if someone might arrive to help him out. One blow, properly placed, could kill him now.

II. Paternity

So: Stephen Gardiner. Going out, as he's coming in. It's wet, and for a night in April, unseasonably warm, but Gardiner wears furs, which look like oily and dense black feathers; he stands now, ruffling them, gathering his clothes about his tall straight person like black angel's wings.

III. At Austin Friars

Lizzie is still up. When she hears the servants let him in, she comes out with his little dog under her arm, fighting and squealing. "Forget where you lived?"

Part Two

I. Visitation

They are taking apart the cardinal's house. Room by room, the king's men are stripping York Place of its owner. They are bundling up parchments and scrolls, missals and memoranda and the volumes of his personal accounts; they are taking even the ink and the quills. They are prizing from the walls the boards on which the cardinal's coat of arms is painted.

II. An Occult History of Britain

Once, in ten days of time immemorial, there was a king of Greece who had thirty-three daughters. Each of these daughters rose up in revolt and murdered her husband. Perplexed as to how he had bred such rebels, but not wanting to kill his own flesh and blood, their princely father exiled them and set them adrift in a rudderless ship.

Structural cues in chapter 1 of *The Wind-Up Bird Chronicle* by Haruki Murakami

Murakami is very clear about what he is doing in his text: using scene, exposition, commentary. You can see his approach by looking at the first chapter. He uses a dot to shift from one narrative component to another. I'm just going to observe what each section, dot to dot, is made up of in this chapter. My notes comprise a very short *scenario*.

Scene: The chapter opens with a scene—the narrator is cooking when the phone rings. It continues for some pages in a sequence of activities ending with his resolve to go look for a lost cat.

Exposition: After the dot, the narrator tells about quitting his job, why he did so, his wife's reaction, and so on. He ends with the sentence: "And so I quit my job."

Scene: He returns to a scene at his apartment, and there is another phone call from a seductive stranger.

Exposition, nested in a scene: In the next passage he climbs over a wall into an alley. He explains the story of the alley, what it is. He describes houses, gardens, etc., and after a couple of pages of description, segues into a scene where he sees a girl in a garden and engages with her about the cat until she leaves to get a drink.

Scene: There is a break and we return to a scene when the girl comes back with her Coke. There is a long scene with her. All of this is dialogue.

Scene: The next passage begins, "When I woke up, I was alone. The girl had disappeared."

Scene, interiority: In the next very short passage, he is home again preparing dinner. He has the idea to write a poem about a wind-up bird.

Scene, interiority: His wife comes home. The discussion of the missing cat goes on. The words of a poem come to him. The phone rings again.

My description of course does not do justice to the author's writing, but I hope it makes the point that it is very clear in its layout of narrative components. He uses an obvious cue to the reader that he is shifting scenes or intention: he inserts a dot.

This might be overly simplistic for you. Too obvious. But it might, as an exercise, help you sort out a jumble of text. You could use your own symbol to separate text where there is a change of narrative strategy. Later perhaps you would remove the symbol and use white space. Or not use a signal at all. What would really matter is that you would become acutely conscious of what you did in each segment of the text, such as:

Convey a scene of dialogue and action.

Tell something about a character's history.

Describe the surroundings through which the character is walking.

Return to scene.

Then you could evaluate the clarity of your shifts and the balance of the strategies.

Exercises

See if you can go through a chapter of your own and "insert your dots," indicating shifts in narrative strategy. If not, why not? Is your text muddled? Or elegantly woven? All that matters is that the reader can follow the lines of thought and action.

❏ Choose a favorite scene and write a sentence describing the need or desire of the point of view (POV) character. How are you made aware of it? Overtly (in dialogue or in character thought) or by actions? How does the scene desire tie into the overall character journey?

❏ Choose a chapter that has more than one scene. Is it clear where each scene begins and ends? How does the author move the story in between scenes?

❑ Is there a writer you like whose work is highly imagistic, conveying sensory impressions and emotions through description? Choose a passage and make a list of the images that are included.

Raymie Nightingale by Kate DiCamillo: Story problems; synopsis

I was looking for a book for my granddaughter. When I read the flyleaf for this book I realized that it was a perfect example of how a novel has to have a *big* goal (here, getting her father to come back home) and a *short-term* or *along-the-way* goal (here, winning the Little Miss Central Florida Tire competition). In fact, this come-hither text on the book jacket lays out the story problems (big and short term), establishes the obstacles, and announces the satisfactory outcome!

You wouldn't want to tell an adult reader everything that is going to happen like this, but you couldn't go wrong trying to write a similar synopsis for your own use. The main thing is to have control of the structure, and DiCamillo is a great model.

Here is the text from the flyleaf.

Raymie Clarke has come to realize that everything, absolutely everything, depends on her. And she has a plan. If Raymie can win the Little Miss Central Florida Tire competition, then her father, who left town two days ago with a dental hygienist, will see Raymie's picture in the paper and (maybe) come home. To win, not only does Raymie have to do good deeds and learn how to twirl a baton; she also has to contend with the wispy, frequently fainting Louisiana Elefante, who has a show-business background, and the fiery, stubborn Beverly Tapinski, who's determined to sabotage the contest. But as the competition approaches, loneliness, loss, and unanswerable questions draw the three girls into an unlikely friendship—and challenge each of them to come to the rescue in unexpected ways.

Separating action from commentary in *The Stranger* by Albert Camus

If you do study this book, just focus first on *what happens*. Maybe underline all the sentences of action (as opposed to description or commentary). Much of the book is Meursault's contemplation of his mother's death, of what he did and what will happen to him, and, ultimately, his understanding of death. But there is definitely a chain of scenes holding the book together, taking this character from his mother's funeral to the cell where he awaits the guillotine, and it's good practice to tease out the action from the commentary. Also important for your study would be to write aboutness statements and to think about the power of the setting.

If you are feeling up to a challenge, go through the book page by page and make a list of the topics of Meursault's introspection. You will see that there are categories, so group them. Once you have done the survey, go back through the passages and see what changes have occurred in his thinking. This, after all, is what the book is about: Meursault's perception of his world.

Scene development and backstory in *Benediction* by Kent Haruf

This book is simply constructed of scene after scene. There is, however, an affecting backstory—Dad Lewis's estrangement from his beloved son. Lewis has terminal cancer and he is waiting to die, but the subplot of his need to tell his son farewell is a strong thread through the vigil. Meanwhile, even in such a quiet place, there are things happening that subtly move life forward for family and the community, as Lewis's life is ending.

This would be a very good introduction to storyboarding, if you want; it is worth studying as a model of integrating a straightforward plot with a powerful subtext of a son's absence.

Motifs in Mark Haddon's *The Curious Incident of the Dog in the Night-Time*

This is a fun book and it won't be especially difficult to write out a chain of scenes. Watch how each thing that Christopher learns marks a kind of turn in his quest and modifies his goal. You could also write a chain of topics that Christopher talks about as he explains how he goes about living his life and solving problems. Either way, you would see a logical sequence winding through the story.

Another way to analyze the story might be instructive because it would make you lay out the scenes a different way. Think of the themes or motifs that exist because of Christopher's special makeup. Make strings of scenes according to themes; obviously scenes will appear in more than one string. For example, look at the ways that Christopher struggles to do things on his own, and keep in mind his ultimate goal of passing his A-level math exam. To do this, watch for the ways that he expresses discomfort and frustration *and then does something about it.*

You would also understand the novel on another level if you went through it and noted all the ways that his life is interrupted and made difficult by the failures of others to do things in logical, orderly ways. How does he deal with them? Sometimes he has to actually *do* something, such as when he makes his way through London. But at other times he deals with his frustration by thinking about topics that allow him to review the way some things work very logically, according to rules. All of these threads—actions and topics and responses—are woven into the story expertly. And you can find threads other than these I have named.

Aboutness in Ernest J. Gaines's *A Lesson Before Dying*

This would be a terrific book to study for its development of the two parts of the aboutness statement: what happens as the sequence of events; what happens emotionally, thematically, and how it affects the protagonist. Grant Wiggins has been talked into visiting Jefferson, a young man unjustly convicted of murder and sentenced to die, with the goal of helping him die "with dignity." In other words, Grant has the formidable goal of helping a very young, frightened, and angry boy accept his fate. The novel has two distinct story lines: the interaction of Grant and Jefferson; and Grant's own life, wherein his bitterness and lack of faith have kept him from deep relationships and a meaningful sense of his own work and worth. Define and describe the two lines of development and watch how each man influences the other. It's such an amazing novel, an opportunity to see how a great novel portrays the growth of a boy into a brave man, and a bitter, depressed man into a person with hope of finding meaning in his life.

Sample Scenarios

Chapter 29 of *Benediction* by Kent Haruf

The chapter is divided by blocks of white space between sections, to indicate changes of scene. I have numbered these for the convenience of my summary; there are no numbers in the text. I include here the first sentence of each section, followed by my summary of subsequent events.

CHAPTER TAGLINE: LORRAINE, Berta May, and the neighbor girl Alice go out to the Johnson house to spend an afternoon picnicking and swimming.

What "happens" in the chapter: Little Alice is brought into the world of women's friendship.

1. "A little while before noon on a day earlier in that same week, Lorraine went next door to Berta May's and then she and Alice came out and drove east on U.S.

Highway 34, then south on the gravel to the Johnson house."

The women are greeted by the Johnson women, Willa and Alene, and embraced.

2. "They ate lunch in the yard on the north side of the house under an elm tree."

They say grace, with special mention of the young girl, and then they eat.

3. "They passed the dishes around."

Alice goes indoors and checks things out and then they all decide on a nap. Alice goes in again, to get some bedspreads.

4. "They lay out on the ground in the shade of the tree, with dinner napkins draped over their faces, to ward off the flies."

They talk about music. Willa tells a story about not practicing, as a child, then she falls asleep. Alice falls asleep, too.

5. "We ought to go swimming, Lorraine said. I wish there was a creek out here."

The three women and the girl put away the things from their picnic. Then they walk out into the pasture to a tank with fresh cold water. Soon they all take their clothes off and get in, although Willa (the old woman) has to be coaxed. When they learn that Alice can't swim, they help her float.

6. "After a time they got out and sat in the lawn chairs, facing the sun."

The cows come in the pasture to get a drink and see what's going on. The women talk about the cows, what it's like to be a milk cow, and make jokes about being women. Then they all get back in the tank and float, then stand up, wet and shining. After that they take everything back to the house.

Summary notes from *Opal on Dry Ground*

As I mentioned in the text, I often wrote summaries of chapters or chapter sequences before I wrote the actual text. So here are some of my notes, somewhere in the middle of the book. No editing, no fussing, this was just put-it-down stuff. By writing out the line of the plot, I had less to invent as I was writing.

CLANCY HAS TAKEN a lover, a cotton farmer she met at the bank, where he is a good customer. Travis is a thirty-one-year-old kid, lusty and silly. He makes her angry and giddy. She wants equilibrium, and Travis scares and confuses her.

One day after work she goes to the hospital with a coworker and is smitten with the preemies in the nursery. She imagines herself a nurse but is overwhelmed at the thought of going back to school. When she mentions it to her mother, though, Opal runs around getting catalogs, killing Clancy's enthusiasm.

Joy, meanwhile, has not found regular employment. Her sources of income include selling snow cones at the flea market and typing college papers. She dates men she meets in bars and one morning she wakes up with a black eye; that same morning her daughter Heather calls from Amarillo begging her to come get her. Heather is miserable at her father's house, where there is a second wife and a new baby. So Joy goes to get her, and on the way back tells her a long story about her own childhood, explaining some of her anger toward men.

Meanwhile, Opal's husband, Russell, is working a pipeline in New Mexico. Opal has gone to visit him in his crummy little trailer and he is pressuring her to go around with him where work takes him. She claims she can't live in a little trailer, but they both know the reason she isn't with Russell is that she won't leave Clancy. Russell doesn't mind that his stepdaughters live in his house; in fact, his idea is, leave them in it. He makes

Opal's choice concrete; he buys a nice new trailer. Opal agrees to go with him on his next job.

Soon after, Russell takes them all, with dates, to a western dance club. He and Joy have a good time but Clancy feels ill, so of course Opal takes her home. It turns out she's pregnant, and so Opal tells Russell she can't go with him to Mineral Wells. He blows up and says, Fine, stay here and have Clancy's baby with her. I'm going to Africa.

Notes on my revision scheme for *A Chance to See Egypt*

I thought it might be interesting for you to see my interpretation of an "outline" as I was preparing to revise this novel. I had spent a lot of time working on the story before I wrote it—months, really—while I was taking care of a sick family member. So when I wrote the first draft I had a good grasp of story and my intention. I wanted to write a novel that was a little bit like a European tale, in which characters are slightly "flat," playing out roles as in a play. I wanted a happy story. I had been through months of worry, and I undertook this enterprise very deliberately to remind myself—and the world?—that happiness is possible. So there is a lightness and inevitability-of-good in it. A fairy-tale quality. At the same time, of course, I wanted there to be real story problems, and characters who suffered and were in some way transformed.

Instead of a straight summary or sequence, I laid the "outline" down on a large sheet of paper and put it up on the wall before me as I retyped the manuscript. Here it is.

A Chance to See Egypt

Main Plot

A grieving man (Riley) returns to the town of his honeymoon. Befriended by an American writer (Charlotte), he ventures out. In small steps, he overcomes his timidity.

He meets a woman (Cruz) and her daughter (Divina)
and is drawn to their mystery, strength, beauty,
and domesticity. The friendship challenges
convention and draws the ire of other vacationing
Americans.

He moves to the women's village and courts the mother,
even as the daughter courts him. Passion ignited, he is
tormented by doubt, and resists the direction of his love.
He proposes to the mother, who says no.

At a fiesta, he dances with the mother, but when her secret
love steps forward, he turns to the daughter to dance.
When they kiss, he bolts.

He spends the night in the chapel with the priest (Father
Bernal).

In the morning he emerges into the light.

The American woman takes him to the girl at work. He
declares his love of her before everyone.

They are married at a wedding to which the whole village is
invited.

A circus appears. Still in wedding clothes, the couple ride
an elephant.

Subplots

Charlotte. The American woman is hiding from her own
life. She writes at night. She paints in black and white!
She spends herself on others' stories: Cruz's story, told at
night; Divina's dreams of a white house; the retirees'
memories. She is the mistress of an absentee don. Her
only confidant is the priest. She learns the very thing she
tells Riley: To feel is strength. As Riley's grief is ending,
she embraces her own grief about her dead child and her
abandoned art.

Father Bernal. The priest struggles with his own dark night.
(He secretly, chastely loves Charlotte.)

Cruz. A proud independent woman who prays for her son Berto to come home for the fiesta and for her daughter to marry well. She wants affirmation of the worthiness of her story. She tells it to her daughter in lessons, and as promises. Then she tells her, "I will tell you the story of Senor Riley and Divina." She has long been the secret lover of the widower Don Genaro, a grocer and descendant of the old hacienda family. At the end he comes forward and gives Divina away at her wedding.

Divina. Pretty, proud, yearning. As Riley once looked to his wife for direction in his life, Divina now looks to Riley. She admires his experience, his tales of travel. She delights in his work—the idea of owning a pet store! She thinks his red hair is wonderful. And the priest says he is a good man.

Eusebio longs to leave—with Divina—but when he sees that he will never marry her, and the circus comes, he seizes the day.

Yzelda loves the village and would never leave, but pines for Reymundo, who left on a water truck. When he appears with the circus, he stays.

Riley's sister *Margaret* is apoplectic when he extends his stay. She sends her son as envoy. He arrives and stays for the wedding.

The grocer *Don Genaro* thinks Riley is going to marry Cruz, and this worry brings him out of his shyness and secrecy.

The lessons each character teaches Riley:

Eva (his dead wife): Journey to the sacred to be made whole.

Consolata: Healing stories lie in our shadows.

Charlotte: To feel is to be strong.

Father Bernal: The open heart is filled.

Riley is a man who embraces his *anima*. He loves the female for her strength and beauty.

———

HERE IS A page from an earlier stage of planning.

Subject: A timid lonely man looks for love and courage.
Themes: Faith and grace; love as sacrament available to all.
Premise: The heart that opens is filled.
The journey through the dark leads to the light.

Main Characters

Tom Riley wants release from grief and loneliness. He wants family. He doesn't know if he has enough courage to love again. Can he yield to mystery?

Divina is a kind of Cinderella, held in place by lack of opportunity. She wants a castle; her dream is to be a maid in a gringo house in Texas. Never having had a father, she is drawn to Riley, though he is not old enough to be her parent. In time, she sees him as a prince and the holder of the key to what she wants. Can she win him? Is it the right thing to do?

Cruz wants her children to have a better life than she has had. She wants grandchildren. She wants her Indian blood to survive.

Minor Characters

Margaret (Riley's sister) wants the world to stand still.

Charlotte (the American writer) wants to transcend herself as a woman and as an artist, but she has to face the truth of her mediocre talent.

The priest wants a mystical experience.

The guests at the hotel form a chorus with two songs: "Go for it, Riley!" and "Don't be an old fool!"

———

WITH ALL THESE notes, I made a sort of tree of characters and used shorthand phrases to represent scenes. Then I started writing scene sequences on index cards, arranging and rearranging their order. I spent a lot of time thinking about images: Divina with her long hair; Riley on the elephant; Charlotte at her easel; and so on. I was able to spend a couple weeks in Mexico, and I took dozens of photographs that provided small details—birds in cages, certain foods on a grill, a small band in a square, etc.

As I wrote, I had photographs taped up on the wall, as well as my index cards on strings.

Storyboarding

THE FIRST THING you want to do is choose a novel you like and know well, and that isn't overly complicated or long, and study it as a model. *Evergreen*, by Rebecca Rasmussen, has an accessible structure. Evan S. Connell's *Mrs. Bridge* is an interesting choice because it is written in vignettes, with numerous strands. If you write with a lot of interiority, consider *Tinkers*, by Paul Harding. *Breathing Lessons*, by Anne Tyler, lends itself well to this exercise, though any of her novels would serve. Other suggestions: any novel by Kaye Gibbons; *Drowning Ruth*, by Christina Schwarz; anything by Elizabeth Berg. For emphasis on themes, *Breath, Eyes, Memory*, by Edwidge Danticat; *House of Sand and Fog*, by Andre Dubus III; J. M. Coetzee's *Disgrace*; Bernhard Schlink's *The Reader*; Ernest J. Gaines's *A Lesson Before Dying*. Really, study what interests you, but start with a book that doesn't seem overwhelming. If you are interested in a particular genre, obviously you'll want to study a book that represents the approach you want to take for science fiction, mystery, young adult, multigenerational fiction, and so on. Work to understand the overall structure of the book. Later, you can choose favorite chapters and analyze them for structure. You could go on to look at more books by analyzing the opening chapters and then some from deeper in the story. You want to internalize the way stories are shaped.

You will need two different colors of index cards and some Post-it Notes.

1. Go through and write taglines for the chapters.

    Then write out an index card for each chapter and put the tagline on it.

    You can now lay out the chapter cards horizontally on the wall, the floor, a bulletin board, a large swath of paper, etc. You will be putting more cards about each chapter below these.

2. For each chapter, identify the scenes. Put the number of the chapter that the scene appears in.

    Write an index card for each scene in the main plot: a one-sentence summary of the action of the scene; setting; characters. If the scene raises a significant question, write the question out at the bottom of the card.

    If there is a significant amount of flashback or exposition or narrative summary, make a card and label it for the type of text it is: **FB** (flashback), **EX** (exposition), **NS** (narrative summary), and write a caption that summarizes it. For example: memories of the flood; summary of the week in the hospital; an explanation of where the father has been and why he has returned.

    Put the scene cards in a string below the chapter tagline cards.

    Do a *separate string of cards* just like this for any subplot. Use a different color for each subplot, or draw a thick colored line across the top of the card, a color for each subplot.

3. I have seen writers hang their storyboards with string, but having the cards on a surface means you can write on them, adding notes as things occur to you.

Also, you can take a felt pen and make lines from one scene to a scene in another chapter, to show that they are connected in the plot.

4. Study your scene cards and decide how they "clump" into scene sequences. You can indicate this by moving the scene cards closer together, perhaps abutting one another, with some space before you move to the next scene sequence. Note that sometimes a scene sequence will "spill over" into the next chapter.

5. Decide which scenes matter most, which ones are major events, and with a felt pen, put a big star on the card, or draw around it like a frame. You want to be able to stand and look at the storyboard and follow different elements, depending on what you are thinking about.

"Here is the line of major events."

"There's the subplot about the brother's divorce."

Identify all the ways you can that the novel connects: settings, story questions, backstory, motifs like loneliness, blood, etc.

As you work on developing your own scene sequences you will have a visual template to rely on for structure.

THE IDEA, OBVIOUSLY, is to spend this much time taking a book apart so that you get a good idea of how it was put together. You want to see for yourself that a book is made up of components, pieces that go together in small bunches that go together in larger ones, that add up to the whole story. It's dissection.

When you later are working on your own novel, use elements of this exercise to build your own picture of your novel's structure. Since you are writing on cards that can be moved around or replaced or deleted, you have lots of flexibility as you go deeper into the story and recognize things that should have happened earlier, or should have been different. Personally, I find this way of working to be a welcome change from the "sit down at the computer" approach day in and day out. It's a lot of fun to see a story take shape, and it's helpful to organize the skeleton of the novel.

I suggest starting with a novel that is made up of many scenes, rather than one dense with narrative summary. A short novel! Mysteries work well. But if you are working on something complex like a historical novel or a novel with multiple plotlines, you should do a storyboard for a novel like your own in structure. It will be challenging, and you will have to work out your own scheme for indicating the many different parts, but if you can do it for something already written, you'll find it a lot easier to do it for your novel.

An illustration of storyboarding

I am working on a novel, currently called *Staph*. In a matter of six weeks, both parents of two adolescent sisters die, the first of a staph infection and the second of myocarditis (an infection of the lining of the heart). The girls, Mia (age fourteen) and Annika (thirteen), have been leading an unusually sheltered life and have been out of school most of the year (the book opens in March). Subtle undercurrents in the novel suggest that, really, the girls are better off; their parents lived strangely, smoked marijuana regularly, and kept their daughters too close.

The book is about how the extended family manages to bear the shock and grief of the losses, while providing a wholesome and optimistic environment for the girls. Recovery. Growth. Family love. And the blossoming of young girls into teenagers.

Of course that's what everyone thinks is happening. The girls get their own beds; they get new clothes; they are enrolled in school in the town where their father's mother lives, and spend time with their other grandmother, too. Their aunt and cousin also live in their grandmother's house, though the aunt, Alison, had been planning to remarry soon.

The story is really about the girls. They have been raised like twins, never apart, but in their new environment they learn more about who they are as individuals, and they make different choices about how to begin building their orphaned lives. Annika, the younger girl, is mentored by a math teacher and a track coach, and makes an unusual friendship with an immigrant family. Her older sister, Mia, however, has been yearning to be out in the world. She rushes into a circle of friendships, though her special pal is the troubled son of her aunt's boyfriend. She doesn't care about school; she cares about belonging, and about not being a little girl anymore.

Nobody except Annika sees that Mia isn't doing well in school and is getting out of her league with her peers; and Annika doesn't want to trample on her own good luck by trying to interfere with Mia's bad behavior. Besides, she doesn't know how to make Mia behave. And it's not her job.

In this way, Mia—along with some of her peers—loses control, so that what was supposed to be fun becomes dangerous. And the adults—each of whom has her own story, of course—have to pay closer attention, make new decisions, and guide their children.

So I'm juggling all kinds of characters and their desires and their weaknesses; that's what novels do. I have a lot of pages and a pretty clear structure. It's a good time for me to figure out, step by step, just what stays, what goes, what gets newly written.

The novel is divided into four parts. What I've laid out here is the first part, so that I can follow the flow of the scenes. I've laid out four scene sequences and notes about the scenes within each sequence. These notes would be on index cards, so that I could lay them out and look at them something like I can on the page now, but also I could stack them, make additional notes, etc. Even though it's a little awkward to present my sequences on the pages, I think you can see how I have pinned down the essentials of what, in manuscript, is about forty pages.

Staph: A Novel

Note: My chapters aren't numbered. The book is broken into four "movements," within which scenes or scene sequences are grouped. I have titled and numbered each scene sequence. Line rules indicate changes of scene.

**First Movement:
From Britt's Illness to Her Burial**

1. The day of Mama's illness and the next morning: Britt is stricken with staph infection

Near Portland, Oregon

The girls hang out with Mama: watch TV, play with QVC jewelry.
Mama (Britt) goes to bed, sick.
Girls (Mia, 14; Annika, 13) go to bed.
Mama howling in a.m.
Daddy (Nick) comes home, calls 911; ambulance.
WHAT IS WRONG WITH HER?

Girls play with jewelry and credit cards.
Daddy comes home, doesn't talk, goes to bed.
Girls play with jewelry, lie down, arms out like angel wings.
IS MAMA DEAD?

Exposition: What life is like in the shabby apartment
Next a.m.: Nick is gone.

Girls go to McDonald's.

Back home, they bounce volleyball against garage; encounter nosy woman asking why they're not in school.

Nick has returned but is asleep and won't wake.

Someone calls for him, avoids saying who it is, but it is about Mama.

Girls try to wake up Nick, finally call their grandmother Willow.

IS MAMA DEAD?

Backstory: How Nick and Britt met

Nick was a pharmacist in Frost, Britt's hometown; they worked in a grocery store.

(scene) She came to him for help with her insomnia.

He took her out to eat and then home, and taught her how to smoke weed. It was Kismet.

---

2. The grandmothers appear and move the family out of the apartment

Southern Oregon and Then Portland

Willow (Nick's mother) has to go tell Johanna (Britt's mother) that Britt is dead. Johanna slaps Willow in shock.

They have coffee and talk about what to do. Johanna wants to manage the burial in her family plot. Willow calls the funeral director.

The women drive to Portland, no conversation.
Backstory: Johanna thinks about Britt's illness last fall when she was bitten by a bat

They arrive at the apartment. It is dirty, fetid, trashy. Nick in bed, girls on couch. Johanna falls to her knees; Willow kneels beside her. The girls stand up and watch, curious.

Willow goes into motion: She wakes Nick. She tells him he has to tell the children their mother is dead. She makes ice water.
The girls are sitting beside Johanna.
Nick comes out and tries to explain Britt's death.
Willow takes over and says how things are going to go: Nick and Johanna have to go to make arrangements with the funeral home. Willow will get food. Everyone but Nick will go to a motel for the night.

Willow helps the girls sort some clothes, leaving a lot behind. They pack their mother's jewelry.

At the motel the girls sleep in Johanna's room. Willow tries to reassure the girls: They are all going to Willow's home. They will all be together. WHAT IS GOING TO HAPPEN TO THE FAMILY NOW?

In the apt Nick sleeps and dreams.

Backstory: The time at the coast when they got stoned and imagined aliens would come for them

---

Nick and Willow clear out the apartment and pay the manager to dispose of all the trash. Nick finds a shoebox with the family's important papers.

---

3. Willow and her daughter Alison make their way to Britt's burial, stopping to leave Alison's daughter at her dad's

Nick had left early to go to Johanna's place. (The grave is on Sunderson property.) The girls are already there, with their grandmother.

Willow and Alison eat breakfast and discuss what will become of Nick without Britt. Willow worries about fitting everybody in her house. Alison is optimistic and practical. Things will work out.

Her daughter Fiona, age 6, appears.

Exposition: Fiona's father, Ben, is a doctor who lives in the next town. Her parents so far have done okay with the back and forth. Alison isn't crazy about her ex's religious wife and the family's Baby Jesus talk. Willow bemoans her son's lack of ambition.

At Ben's house, he starts an argument with Alison over her tardiness and her general attitude about his parental rights. Alison, who is surprised, reminds him they are going to a funeral. But now she's worried.

Ben says, "Nick should have asked for an autopsy."
IS TROUBLE BREWING FOR BEN AND ALISON?

---

4. The burial and its aftermath
Simple gravesite ceremony: Johanna, her brother, and
her sister-in-law; Nick and the girls; Willow and
Alison; a neighbor; and a friend of Britt's from high
school. The Lutheran minister speaks briefly.

At Johanna's house her brother tells some
stories about Britt and his boys as kids. There is
simple food. People leave. Mia collapses, pounding
the floor.
Nick sends his mother and sister home; he will stay at
Johanna's.

Nick takes the girls to a miniature golf course in
the nearby town. They play. Then they go to a
park and shoot baskets.
They drive back to Frost, on to a small park near
Sunderson property. They are so tired, they all fall
asleep. At twilight, Nick wakes up and takes them to
Johanna's.
HOW WILL THEY SURVIVE BRITT'S DEATH? CAN
THEY HOLD ONE ANOTHER UP AND TOGETHER?

Scene Template

ADAPTED FROM *The Scene Book: A Primer for the Fiction Writer*

I.

Start by asking yourself these fundamental questions:

1. What is the *event* in the scene, and what emotions are connected to it? Does it merit a scene or could it just be summarized?
2. What did you want the scene to accomplish for the story, and does it reach this goal? Caption the *function* of the scene with a word from this list: Revelation, Confrontation, Decision, Information, Recognition, Catalyst, Reflection, Turning Point, Capitulation, Resolution.
3. Is it clear where the scene begins and ends?
4. What is the *pulse* of the scene; is it sufficient to drive the action? Does it accelerate in the scene?

If you think your scene has a problem and you don't see what it is, below are more questions for you to consider.

II.

1. Is the event clear? Try framing it as an aboutness statement. Look for the reason for the scene's drama.

2. Are the beats of action clear? Write them out, one after the other, to check for stammers or repetitions.

3. Does the protagonist have a clear intention in the scene? Does it drive the drama?

4. Does the scene lack subtlety? Maybe you give it all away too soon. Think of the scene as having a question in the first part, with the answer after that.

5. Is the grounding sufficient? Can we tell where your characters are, what's around them? Integrate description and activity without overstating either.

6. How's the dialogue? Try writing it out like a play without action or description so that the voices are isolated. Can you "hear" the difference in characters? Is one personality stronger than another?

7. Does the scene have a strong focal point? This is the place where the scene merges its meaning. If a scene adds up, we are in a different place at the end from where we were when it started. Are we?

If you work hard to make your scenes strong, you'll give your novel muscle. And scene writing will get easier.

Acknowledgments

I am grateful to the writers who participated in classes and workshops with me over many years at the Iowa Summer Writing Festivals; at the Seattle Pacific University MFA residencies; and in the Pine Manor College Solstice MFA program: for their enthusiasm; for their goodwill and generosity with one another; for their persistence and faith in writing. My life has been enriched by the joy of teaching—and learning—with other writers. And I thank the directors who made it possible for me to teach: Peggy Houston, Amy Margolis, Gregory Wolfe, and Meg Kearney.

Thanks to my agent and friend, Emma Sweeney, for encouraging me to undertake this project, and to my husband, Bill Ferguson, for holding up under my flood of talk about it over many months. I am thrilled to work with Carole DeSanti, Christopher Russell, and the other magicians at Viking Penguin who make a manuscript into a book.

The Scene Book

A Primer for the Fiction Writer

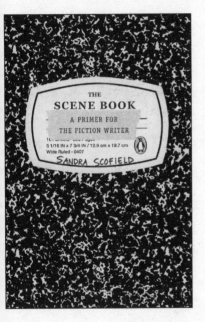

A treasure-trove of writing wisdom from award-winning author and teacher Sandra Scofield, *The Scene Book* is a fundamental guide to crafting more effective scenes in fiction. In clear, simple language, Scofield shows both the beginner and the seasoned writer how to build the kinds of scenes that form the underpinning of any great narrative.

PENGUIN BOOKS